7 YEAR APOCALYPSE

Michael Snyder

CONTENTS

BLOOD ON THE DOORSTEP

On the morning of November 1st, 2020 I woke up with a sense of tremendous urgency. Once again, I had just had the same extremely powerful dream that I had been having night after night, but this time I felt certain that I needed to share what I had been shown with the world.

Up to that point, I had not shared the dream with anyone. In fact, I had not even told my wife about it.

Most of the time I do not share what I see in my dreams with anyone. But this time was different. I didn't fully understand what I had been shown, but I knew that it was a very sobering message about our future.

From a very early age, I have been having "unusual dreams", and throughout my life events that I have seen in my dreams have come to pass over and over again.

In almost all cases, I don't know when the events will happen in advance, and there are times when the dreams are highly symbolic.

But even though my dreams can by very mysterious, I have learned that I should definitely not ignore them. In this book I am going to share some of the end times dreams that I have had in recent months, and one of them has already been fulfilled very specifically.

As I detailed in my last book, it is not unusual for God to speak to His people through dreams, and dreams that are particularly important can sometimes be repeated multiple times.

Over the years, there have been many instances in which the exact same dream has been given to me on multiple occasions, and this happened to me once again in the days leading up to the 2020 presidential election.

In this case, the dreams were incredibly vivid, and they involved blood.

At first I didn't share the repeating dreams with anyone, and I didn't plan to ever share them with anyone.

But then as I slept in the early morning hours of November 1st, I had the same dream again, but it was in the context of a larger dream. And it was what I saw in that larger dream that ultimately motivated me to share the dream with all of you.

After I awakened on the morning of November 1st, the following is what I wrote after I raced over to my computer...

For approximately two weeks, every night I have been having a very unusual dream. I am in a major U.S. city in the dream, and so it is not where I normally live. In the dream, I open the front door of the place where I am staying, and right outside there is blood on the doorstep. The blood is never on me or on anyone inside the place where I am living. But it is completely covering the doorstep outside.

Last night, I saw the same exact thing, but it was within the context of a larger dream in which I was a talk radio host. In that role as a talk radio host, I was talking about the blood on the doorstep, and I am taking this as a sign that I am supposed to share these dreams with the public.

I do not know exactly what these dreams mean or when they will be fulfilled. But I do feel an urgency to share them with all of you today.

Every night it had been the exact same thing.

I would open the front door and I would see red blood completely covering the doorstep. The blood was thick, and there was not a single square inch of the doorstep that was not covered.

But it didn't end there. The blood covered areas well beyond the doorstep as well, and I didn't see where the blood actually ended.

What was beyond the doorstep was not the focus of the dream. My focus was always on the doorstep itself, although I was aware that blood had drenched the entire area.

After I shared this with the world on November 1st, I didn't have the dream again.

I believe that this is a sign that I did what I needed to do.

So what does the dream mean?

That puzzled me for a long time. I asked my readers for their thoughts, and I received some interesting feedback. But it took quite a while before things started to become clear.

Obviously, blood is a very troubling sign. Blood is associated with violence, death and war among other things.

I was encouraged that the blood was never on me, and in the dream I understood that the blood did not belong to me or those that were close to me.

But I was definitely alarmed by what I had been shown, and I wanted to know what it meant.

In the aftermath of the election in November, blood was shed during the storming of the U.S. Capitol, and there was some violence in various cities where there were clashes between the left and the right. But even though those events were "unusual" and even though they occurred very quickly after my repeating dreams, I do not believe that was why I had those dreams.

Another "unusual" thing that happened immediately after the election in November was that the U.S. experienced a surge of COVID cases and COVID deaths like we have never seen before. In fact, the number of COVID deaths went from about a thousand a day at the time of the dreams to more than four thousand a day at the peak.

So could that have been what these dreams were about?

I don't think so.

Since the publication of my last book, the Lord has put a burden on my heart about this book. I knew that it was supposed to be about the end times, but at first I didn't have anything more than that. For months I didn't have a title or a clear direction. But I also felt such an urgency to write it.

I trusted that God would give me what I needed when I needed it, and He always comes through.

As time went on, the Lord made it clear to me that the focus of this book needed to be on the upcoming 7 year Tribulation period, and during a time of prayer I was given "7 Year Apocalypse" as the title of this book.

And this book is ultimately what I believe the repeating dreams were all about.

They weren't about a handful of people dying during election violence.

And they weren't even about thousands upon thousands of people dying during the height of the COVID pandemic.

Instead, I believe that they were about the billions that will die during the 7 year apocalypse that is rapidly approaching.

In fact, I believe that well over 90 percent of the entire population of the world will die during this upcoming 7 year period.

In Matthew 24, Jesus warned us that during the final 7 years before His return we will witness the worst moments in all of human history. There has never been a time like it before, and there will never be a time like it ever again...

21 For then shall be great tribulation, such as was not since the beginning of the world to this time, no, nor ever shall be.

22 And except those days should be shortened, there should no flesh be saved: but for the elect's sake those days shall be shortened.

Did you catch what verse 22 is saying?

Things will eventually get so bad that all life on Earth would be wiped out unless God intervenes.

This is the time in human history that we are rapidly moving toward, and the vast majority of the people in our society are completely and utterly clueless about what is coming.

In fact, even most Christians are completely and utterly clueless about what is coming.

In this book, I am going to detail what you can expect during the 7 year apocalypse, and I am going to explain why I believe that we are very close to that time.

In the repeating dreams that I described earlier in this chapter, the blood was always on the doorstep. When something is on the doorstep, that is an indication that it is close in proximity or time. The phrases "at the door" or "at the doors" are used repeatedly in the Scriptures, and those phrases are often used to point to something that is imminent.

And during the 7 year apocalypse that is coming, we will see more bloodshed than we have ever had in any 7 year period in all of human history. I now believe that is why I kept seeing blood on the doorstep night after night during those dreams.

In my last book entitled *"Lost Prophecies Of The Future Of America"*, I detailed a series of dramatic cataclysms that will deeply affect the United States and the rest of the world in the years ahead. I believe that most of the events that I discussed in that book will take place during the first half of the 7 year apocalypse.

Many of the things that I am going to talk about in this book are extremely frightening, but the goal of this book is not to scare you. God wants us to understand that He knew about all of these things in advance, He is in control, and He has a plan. God specifically placed you at this moment in history for a reason, and He would not have put you here if He didn't think that you could handle it. It is when things are the darkest that the greatest heroes are needed, and many new heroes will be forged during the exceedingly difficult years that are in front of us.

Ultimately, this is a book of hope. Even in the midst of the 7 year apocalypse, I believe that we will see the greatest move of God in all of human history, and that makes this an extremely exciting time for all of us to be alive.

It isn't an accident that you are reading this book. God brought this book to your attention for a purpose, and He has a very specific plan for the next stage of your life. The greatest chapters of your life can still be ahead of you, but you have got to be willing to totally surrender to Him.

One way or another, everything in your life is about to change. You may interpret that statement as bad news, but it doesn't have to be.

The Book of Revelation is a book of great hope. Yes, a lot of bad things are going to happen between now and the return of our Lord and Savior Jesus Christ, but the hope that return gives us far outweighs any temporary trials that we must endure.

A lot of those that do not understand what is ahead are going to plunge into a deep pit of depression once they are blindsided by the cataclysmic events that are coming. But that should not happen. God placed us at this incredibly exciting time in human history for a purpose. My hope is that this book will give you a clear understanding of what is in front of us, and I also hope that it will inspire you to embrace whatever specific purpose God has for your life in this hour.

This will likely be one of the most frightening books that you have ever read, but I also want it to be one of the most uplifting. Ancient prophecies are being fulfilled all around us, and the time of Christ's return is drawing near.

All of the horrible evil that we see in the world today is just temporary. Jesus is going to come back and set everything right, and we are going to live with Him forever.

For those that know Jesus, the end of our story is far greater than anything that Hollywood could ever imagine. But the journey to the final chapter of our story will be filled with chaos and adventure, and once you have finished this book you will clearly understand many of the challenges that we will soon be facing.

TRIBULATION

We are living in the Book of Revelation generation.

During a recent time of prayer, "the Book of Revelation generation" was a phrase that was suddenly dropped into my spirit.
After nearly 2,000 years of waiting, I believe that we will be the
generation that will get to see the events described in the last
book of the Bible play out right in front of our eyes.

The Bible has a tremendous amount to say about the seven year
period just before the return of Jesus. In our day, this period
of time is commonly known by titles such as "the Tribulation",
"the Great Tribulation", "the time of Jacob's trouble" and "Daniel's 70th week". It will be the most apocalyptic stretch of time
in all of human history, and the horrors of this period will be
way beyond what most people would even dare to imagine right
now. In reality, the only time in all of human history that we can
really compare it to would be Noah's Flood. That was one enormous disaster that wiped out nearly all of humanity, but the 7
year apocalypse will be an extended series of disasters and trials
over a 7 year stretch.

Just like Noah's Flood, most of the population of the planet is not
going to survive what is coming.

And just like Noah's Flood, most of the population of the planet
is going to be completely blindsided by the events that are ahead.

We tend to avoid thinking about how short our lives really are,
because most people don't like to think much about death.

But death is coming on a massive scale.

Most of the people living in the world today will enter the 7 year apocalypse, and most of the people living in the world today will not make it through it.

I know that this is a very blunt statement, but a lot of un-believers will read this book, and they need to understand exactly what we are facing.

Life is just temporary, and for a lot of you it is going to be a lot more temporary than you originally thought.

In fact, a lot of people that will read this book will die at a very early age.

Don't wait until tomorrow to turn to God. If you have not done so, invite Jesus Christ into your life to be your Lord and Savior today, because tomorrow is not guaranteed for any of us.

If you do know the Lord but have backslidden, get right with God immediately, because the only way that you are going to have any hope during the years that are ahead is if you are walking closely with the Almighty.

This is a point that I am going to make more than once in this book, and there are other points that I will repeat as well. One of the reasons why I repeat myself so often is because any good teacher knows that one of the keys to learning is repetition, and I want you to walk away from this book with certain principles seared into your mind.

In addition, there are a lot of dots that I need to connect in this book, and so there will be certain passages of Scripture that I will need to come back to repeatedly to show you how they all interconnect.

Bible prophecy is a very complex subject, and I have been study-ing it for more than four decades. When I was a young child, I was fascinated by *The Late Great Planet Earth* by Hal Lindsey, and I have been hooked ever since.

As you read this book, I would like for you to be willing to take a fresh look at the prophetic passages in the Bible about the end times. I am going to directly challenge some of the most com-mon assumptions about Bible prophecy, and that may cause some readers to initially cringe. I would ask that you consider the things that I have to say, and then go and search the Scrip-tures for yourself to see if they are true or not.

Just because you may have been taught something in the past does not mean that it is accurate. The Scriptures are our author-ity, and what we have been taught in the past must be discarded if it does not line up with the Bible.

For example, it is commonly taught that there are two key events that will mark the beginning of the 7 year Tribulation period, but in this book I will show that neither of those things will ac-tually happen at that time.

However, there are three key signs that will let us know that we have entered the 7 year apocalypse, and I will be detailing those in a later chapter.

In the gospels, Jesus repeatedly instructs us to "watch" for signs of His return. Unfortunately, only a very, very small percentage of the population is actively watching for signs of His return today.

The good news is that this is going to change. As the cata-strophic events of the 7 year apocalypse begin to transpire, there will be a greater interest in Bible prophecy than ever before, and we can use this to bring multitudes of souls into the Kingdom.

This is a book that is going to deeply frighten a lot of people, but it is also a book of great hope. The Book of Revelation has an incredibly positive ending, and if you belong to Jesus you will be able to participate in that ending.

But if you have rejected God and you don't ever intend to change your mind, the times that are rapidly approaching will be emotionally devastating for you.

The 7 year apocalypse is going to be beyond challenging. To call those years "nightmarish" would be a major understatement.

If you are living your life just for yourself, the years ahead will be exceptionally painful. Even if you are able to survive, everything that you thought that your life was going to be about will be taken from you. Your plans, your goals, your hopes and your dreams will all be crushed as global events spin wildly out of control. Sooner or later, you will lose most of your material possessions, people that you know will be dying all around you, and the world will seem like it has gone completely insane.

Many of those that do not know Jesus will go mad, many others will plunge into a pit of depression from which they will never recover, and multitudes will end up committing suicide.

But if you choose to live your life for Christ, the years ahead can truly be the best of times.

Yes, there will be a lot of hardships. But if you are living for God, this will be a truly amazing time to be alive.

I believe that we are on the verge of the greatest move of God that the world has ever seen. Even in the midst of all the chaos and all the darkness, God is going to be doing unprecedented things.

In these last days, God is raising up a Remnant that will keep His Commandments, that will preach the gospel to the whole world and fulfill the Great Commission in this generation, and that will move in all of the fruit, all of the gifts and all of the power of the Holy Spirit like we haven't seen since the Book of Acts.

You were born for such a time as this. All of human history has been building up to this moment, and God decided to put you at this time in history for a reason.

Even if you have been disappointed with how your life has turned out so far, the greatest chapters of your life can still be ahead of you and you can still accomplish incredible things for the Kingdom of God.

But in order to do that, you need to be totally sold out for Him.

The Scriptures tell us that the 7 year apocalypse will be divided into two halves. Both halves will be truly horrific, but what most people don't realize is that the second half of the 7 year apocalypse will be vastly different from the first half. In this book, I will explain this in detail.

It is during the second half of the 7 year apocalypse that we will see "the Mark of the Beast", and this is a topic that there has been a tremendous amount of confusion about. Hopefully this book will help to clear things up.

God didn't tell us about all of these things in advance so that we would be afraid.

On the contrary, God told us about all of these things in advance so that we would not fear.

God knew that all of these things would happen. He has a plan, He is in control, and He is going to fulfill His Word to the letter.

Because I write about such hard topics in my articles and in my books, a lot of people assume that I must be depressed.

But I am not depressed at all. I am not on any drugs and I don't have to take anything to make myself happy.

My joy comes from the Lord, and even though I know that we are moving into the most challenging time in all of human history, there is nowhere else that I would rather be than right here, right now.

This book is a call to fight the good fight. It is when times are the darkest that the greatest heroes are needed, and God has a job for you to do.

When our Father sent His Son to die for us on the cross, He gave us His very best.

Are you ready to give your very best to Him?

I understand that a lot of believers out there are afraid to go through what is ahead. Unfortunately, a lot of that comes from bad teaching that they have received in the past.

If God didn't think that you could handle what is ahead, He would not have put you here.

God has a unique purpose for you, although it may be far different from what you originally imagined.

If you ever dreamed of living during biblical times, you are about to get your chance.

The 7 year apocalypse is very close, and the vast majority of the population of the globe is going to be absolutely blindsided by it.

Sadly, very few churches are sounding the alarm, and many preachers carefully avoid ever talking about Bible prophecy because it might scare people away. For many ministries, the most important thing is to keep people coming back week after week so that they will keep putting more money into the offering plate.

This book might offend some people, but I don't care. My job is to warn the people about what is coming, and time for sounding the alarm is rapidly running out.

My books are read by people all over the globe, but the majority of my readers speak English, and so I will be using a lot of terms and phrases that are commonly used among Christians in the English-speaking world. For example, I will be using the name "Jesus" a lot in this book, even though His disciples used the name "Yahshua" (some render it "Yeshua") during His earthly ministry nearly 2,000 years ago. Jesus is an English translation of the Greek translation of Yahshua's name ("Iesous"), and the letter "J" did not even exist until the Middle Ages. But for the purposes of this book, I will be using names for people and places that those that speak English are commonly familiar with.

In future books I may change my approach. It is so important that we understand the history, the language and the culture of first century believers, because a lot of bad doctrines have resulted from removing certain passages in the Bible from their historical and cultural contexts.

Just a few centuries after the time of Jesus, Christians had gotten totally away from doing things the way that the first believers did them. Over time, there have been movements (such as the Protestant reformation) that have helped to turn us back in the right direction, and that process continues today. In fact, I believe that we are now witnessing the final transition of the church. We are finally going to get back to doing things the way that they did them in the first century, and that is going to open a door for great revival.

There are many out there that have assumed that revival would come during an era of great peace and prosperity, but the truth is that it is going to come during a time of great shaking.

Our world is about to be greatly, greatly shaken for a period of 7 years, and all of that shaking will prepare the way for the return of our Lord and Savior.

For those of us that are believers, those are words that should bring us great joy.

But for those that have rejected God, those are words that should absolutely terrify you.

The 7 year apocalypse is rapidly approaching, and nothing will ever be the same again.

"THE 7 YEAR PEACE TREATY WITH ISRAEL"

Being able to correctly identify when the 7 year apocalypse has begun is going to be of the utmost importance, but unfortunately many believers are watching for the wrong signs.

Ever since I was very young, I have been hearing Bible prophecy teachers boldly declare that the Great Tribulation will begin when the Antichrist makes a 7 year peace treaty with Israel. This mantra has been repeated so often in evangelical circles over the years that nobody really questions it anymore.

But is it actually true?

No.

It may surprise you to learn that this entire theory comes from just a single verse in the Bible, and when you examine the original language of that verse the theory quickly falls apart. It is so important for us to embrace what the Bible actually says and not what we would like for it to say. And in this case, a faulty theory could cause many believers to completely misinterpret where we are on God's timeline.

The passage in question is actually one of my favorites. This is what Daniel 9:24-27 says in the King James Version...

24 Seventy weeks are determined upon thy people and upon thy holy city, to finish the transgression, and to make an end of sins, and to make reconciliation for iniquity, and to bring in everlasting right-eousness, and to seal up the vision and prophecy, and to anoint the most Holy.

25 Know therefore and understand, that from the going forth of the commandment to restore and to build Jerusalem unto the Messiah the Prince shall be seven weeks, and threescore and two weeks: the street shall be built again, and the wall, even in troublous times.

26 And after threescore and two weeks shall Messiah be cut off, but not for himself: and the people of the prince that shall come shall destroy the city and the sanctuary; and the end thereof shall be with a flood, and unto the end of the war desolations are determined.

27 And he shall confirm the covenant with many for one week: and in the midst of the week he shall cause the sacrifice and the oblation to cease, and for the overspreading of abominations he shall make it desolate, even until the consummation, and that determined shall be poured upon the desolate.

The weeks referred to in this passage are "weeks of years", and Jesus fulfilled the first portion of this prophecy very precisely when he was crucified exactly 69 "weeks" (483 biblical years) after the order to restore and rebuild Jerusalem was given. A complete examination of this remarkable prophetic fulfillment is beyond the scope of this book, and if you are interested in digging deeper there are many great authors that have written about this.

For the purposes of this chapter, we are going to focus on the second part of the prophecy which deals with Daniel's "70th week". Right now, we are in a "pause" between the 69th and 70th weeks which has lasted almost 2,000 years, but now the 70th week is about to begin.

In verse 27, we are told that "he shall confirm the covenant with many for one week", but in the middle of that week "he shall cause the sacrifice and the oblation to cease".

Most Bible prophecy teachers will tell you that "he" refers to "the prince that shall come" in verse 26.

And that would seem to make sense from just a plain reading of the text. Anyone that reads verse 27 would very naturally come to the conclusion that the Antichrist will be the one that will initiate a covenant for a seven year period and that he will also be the one to break that covenant in the middle of the seven years.

But there is a big problem with that theory.

In the original language, the word "he" is nowhere to be found.

The first section of verse 27 is made up of five Hebrew words in the original language. The first Hebrew word is "gabar", and it means "to confirm" or "to strengthen". Needless to say, you only "confirm" or "strengthen" something that already exists. So nobody should really be jumping to the conclusion that a new "treaty" will be created.

Following "gabar" is the Hebrew word "beriyth". That word is translated as "covenant" throughout English translations of the Scriptures, and in the vast majority of cases "beriyth" refers to the covenant that God has made with Israel.

In fact, that exact same Hebrew word is used earlier in Daniel chapter 9. The following is what Daniel 9:4 says in the King James Version...

And I prayed unto the LORD my God, and made my confession, and said, O Lord, the great and dreadful God, keeping the covenant and mercy to them that love him, and to them that keep his commandments;

19

So if that exact Hebrew word was used for God's covenant with His people earlier in the same chapter, do you think that it is likely to have the same meaning when used later in the chapter?

Of course.

The third Hebrew word used in Daniel 9:27 is "rab" which is often translated as "many" in our English translations.

The fourth Hebrew word in that section is "echad" which means "one", and the fifth Hebrew word is "shabua" which can be translated as "a period of seven days" but more commonly it is translated as "week".

So let's put all of the words together.

A correct translation of the first section of Daniel 9:27 should go something like this...

"The Covenant will be confirmed (or strengthened) with many for one week".

That gives that passage an entirely different flavor, doesn't it?

Translators inserted the word "he" into Daniel 9:27 a total of three different times, and they did that because they thought it made sense.

But the truth is that there is no "he" in the original Hebrew of Daniel 9:27 at all.

And that changes everything.

Instead of a "seven year treaty with the Antichrist", I believe that it is God that will be confirming His covenant with all twelve of the tribes of Israel for the last seven years before the return of Jesus.

In the middle of that seven year period, the Beast (also known as the Antichrist) will desecrate the rebuilt Jewish temple, and the "abomination of desolation" will be a sign that believers are to flee to the mountains. In fact, Jesus specifically warned us about all of this in Matthew 24...

15 When ye therefore shall see the abomination of desolation, spoken of by Daniel the prophet, stand in the holy place, (whoso readeth, let him understand:)

16 Then let them which be in Judaea flee into the mountains:

17 Let him which is on the housetop not come down to take any thing out of his house:

18 Neither let him which is in the field return back to take his clothes.

19 And woe unto them that are with child, and to them that give suck in those days!

20 But pray ye that your flight be not in the winter, neither on the sabbath day:

21 For then shall be great tribulation, such as was not since the beginning of the world to this time, no, nor ever shall be.

2 Thessalonians 2 also talks about the moment when the Antichrist will enter the temple and desecrate it...

Now we beseech you, brethren, by the coming of our Lord Jesus Christ, and by our gathering together unto him,

2 That ye be not soon shaken in mind, or be troubled, neither by spirit, nor by word, nor by letter as from us, as that the day of Christ is at hand.

3 Let no man deceive you by any means: for that day shall not come, except there come a falling away first, and that man of sin be revealed, the son of perdition;

4 Who opposeth and exalteth himself above all that is called God, or that is worshipped; so that he as God sitteth in the temple of God, shewing himself that he is God.

We know from Daniel 9 that this "abomination of desolation" happens right in the middle of the seven year period, and in Matthew 24 Jesus warned that there "shall be great tribulation" from that point forward until He returns.

The good news is that He has promised to return "immediately" after those days of tribulation are completed...

29 Immediately after the tribulation of those days shall the sun be darkened, and the moon shall not give her light, and the stars shall fall from heaven, and the powers of the heavens shall be shaken:

30 And then shall appear the sign of the Son of man in heaven: and then shall all the tribes of the earth mourn, and they shall see the Son of man coming in the clouds of heaven with power and great glory.

Once you put all of the pieces together, God's timeline is exceptionally clear.

Sadly, because of decades of faulty teaching the vast majority of Bible-believing Christians will not believe that the 7 year apocalypse has begun until the Antichrist actually appears.

But nowhere in the Bible does it ever say that the Antichrist will appear at the beginning of the Tribulation. In fact, the Book of

Revelation makes it quite clear that he does not come on the scene until the midway point of the 7 year period.

There are only two places in the entire Bible that people get the idea that the Antichrist appears at the beginning of the Tribulation. The first is Daniel 9:27, and we have already dealt with that.

The second is Revelation 6...

And I saw when the Lamb opened one of the seals, and I heard, as it were the noise of thunder, one of the four beasts saying, Come and see.

2 And I saw, and behold a white horse: and he that sat on him had a bow; and a crown was given unto him: and he went forth conquering, and to conquer.

Of course the Antichrist is not actually mentioned at all in those two verses. Over the years, many Bible teachers have speculated that the Antichrist must be the rider on the white horse because it fits with their theology, and they have passed on that speculation to their followers as "fact".

But we must be very careful to not try to make the Bible say what we want it to say.

It may surprise some people to learn that the Antichrist is never identified by that title in the Book of Revelation. Instead, he is identified by titles such as "the Beast" and "the Beast that ascendeth out of the bottomless pit", and he does not even come on the scene until the sounding of the fifth trumpet in Revelation chapter 9...

And the fifth angel sounded, and I saw a star fall from heaven unto the earth: and to him was given the key of the bottomless pit.

2 And he opened the bottomless pit; and there arose a smoke out of the pit, as the smoke of a great furnace; and the sun and the air were darkened by reason of the smoke of the pit.

3 And there came out of the smoke locusts upon the earth: and unto them was given power, as the scorpions of the earth have power.

4 And it was commanded them that they should not hurt the grass of the earth, neither any green thing, neither any tree; but only those men which have not the seal of God in their foreheads.

5 And to them it was given that they should not kill them, but that they should be tormented five months: and their torment was as the torment of a scorpion, when he striketh a man.

6 And in those days shall men seek death, and shall not find it; and shall desire to die, and death shall flee from them.

7 And the shapes of the locusts were like unto horses prepared unto battle; and on their heads were as it were crowns like gold, and their faces were as the faces of men.

8 And they had hair as the hair of women, and their teeth were as the teeth of lions.

9 And they had breastplates, as it were breastplates of iron; and the sound of their wings was as the sound of chariots of many horses running to battle.

10 And they had tails like unto scorpions, and there were stings in their tails: and their power was to hurt men five months.

11 And they had a king over them, which is the angel of the bottomless pit, whose name in the Hebrew tongue is Abaddon, but in the Greek tongue hath his name Apollyon.

I know that I am quoting some long passages of Scripture, but it is imperative that you see these things in context.

In Revelation 11, we are told that the Beast that ascends out of the bottomless pit will make war against the Two Witnesses once they have completed their testimony, and the Beast will kill them...

3 And I will give power unto my two witnesses, and they shall prophesy a thousand two hundred and threescore days, clothed in sackcloth.

4 These are the two olive trees, and the two candlesticks standing before the God of the earth.

5 And if any man will hurt them, fire proceedeth out of their mouth, and devoureth their enemies: and if any man will hurt them, he must in this manner be killed.

6 These have power to shut heaven, that it rain not in the days of their prophecy: and have power over waters to turn them to blood, and to smite the earth with all plagues, as often as they will.

7 And when they shall have finished their testimony, the beast that ascendeth out of the bottomless pit shall make war against them, and shall overcome them, and kill them.

8 And their dead bodies shall lie in the street of the great city, which spiritually is called Sodom and Egypt, where also our Lord was crucified.

9 And they of the people and kindreds and tongues and nations shall see their dead bodies three days and an half, and shall not suffer their dead bodies to be put in graves.

10 And they that dwell upon the earth shall rejoice over them, and make merry, and shall send gifts one to another; because these two prophets tormented them that dwelt on the earth.

11 And after three days and an half the spirit of life from God entered into them, and they stood upon their feet; and great fear fell upon them which saw them.

12 And they heard a great voice from heaven saying unto them, Come up hither. And they ascended up to heaven in a cloud; and their enemies beheld them.

13 And the same hour was there a great earthquake, and the tenth part of the city fell, and in the earthquake were slain of men seven thousand: and the remnant were affrighted, and gave glory to the God of heaven.

If the Antichrist comes on the scene at the beginning of the 7 year apocalypse, then why would he wait three and a half years to finally kill the Two Witnesses?

That doesn't make any sense at all.

The clear sense of this passage is that once the Beast ascends from the pit one of the very first things that he does is to find the Two Witnesses and kill them.

This happens after the testimony of the Two Witnesses is completed at the midpoint of the Tribulation.

In Revelation 13, we are told that the Beast is given power for 42 months, which is three and a half years. This is what Revelation 13:5-8 says about the Beast in the Modern English Version...

5 He was given a mouth speaking great things and blasphemies. And he was given authority to wage war for forty-two months. 6 He opened his mouth to speak blasphemies against God, to blaspheme His name and His tabernacle and those who dwell in heaven. 7 It was granted to him to wage war with the saints and to overcome them. And authority was given him over every tribe and tongue and nation. 8 All who dwell on the earth will worship him, all whose names have not been written in the Book of Life of the Lamb who was slain from the foundation of the world.

The Scriptures are exceedingly clear about the fact that the Beast is only given three and a half years.

Why can't more people understand this?

Following the passage that I just quoted, "the Beast" is mentioned in 19 more verses in the Book of Revelation...

And deceiveth them that dwell on the earth by the means of those miracles which he had power to do in the sight of the beast; saying to them that dwell on the earth, that they should make an image to the beast, which had the wound by a sword, and did live. (Revelation 13:14)

And he had power to give life unto the image of the beast, that the image of the beast should both speak, and cause that as many as would not worship the image of the beast should be killed. (Revelation 13:15)

And that no man might buy or sell, save he that had the mark, or the name of the beast, or the number of his name. (Revelation 13:17)

Here is wisdom. Let him that hath understanding count the number of the beast: for it is the number of a man; and his number is Six hundred threescore and six. (Revelation 13:18)

And the third angel followed them, saying with a loud voice, If any man worship the beast and his image, and receive his mark in his forehead, or in his hand (Revelation 14:9)

And the smoke of their torment ascendeth up for ever and ever: and they have no rest day nor night, who worship the beast and his image, and whosoever receiveth the mark of his name. (Revelation 14:11)

And I saw as it were a sea of glass mingled with fire: and them that had gotten the victory over the beast, and over his image, and over his mark, and over the number of his name, stand on the sea of glass, having the harps of God. (Revelation 15:2)

And the first went, and poured out his vial upon the earth; and there fell a noisome and grievous sore upon the men which had the mark of the beast, and upon them which worshipped his image. (Revelation 16:2)

And the fifth angel poured out his vial upon the seat of the beast; and his kingdom was full of darkness; and they gnawed their tongues for pain (Revelation 16:10)

And I saw three unclean spirits like frogs come out of the mouth of the dragon, and out of the mouth of the beast, and out of the mouth of the false prophet. (Revelation 16:13)

And the angel said unto me, Wherefore didst thou marvel? I will tell thee the mystery of the woman, and of the beast that carrieth her, which hath the seven heads and ten horns. (Revelation 17:7)

The beast that thou sawest was, and is not; and shall ascend out of the bottomless pit, and go into perdition: and they that dwell on the earth shall wonder, whose names were not written in the book of life from the foundation of the world, when they behold the beast that was, and is not, and yet is. (Revelation 17:8)

And the beast that was, and is not, even he is the eighth, and is of the seven, and goeth into perdition. (Revelation 17:11)

And the ten horns which thou sawest are ten kings, which have received no kingdom as yet; but receive power as kings one hour with the beast. (Revelation 17:12)

These have one mind, and shall give their power and strength unto the beast. (Revelation 17:13)

And the ten horns which thou sawest upon the beast, these shall hate the whore, and shall make her desolate and naked, and shall eat her flesh, and burn her with fire. (Revelation 17:16)

For God hath put in their hearts to fulfil his will, and to agree, and give their kingdom unto the beast, until the words of God shall be fulfilled. (Revelation 17:17)

And I saw the beast, and the kings of the earth, and their armies, gathered together to make war against him that sat on the horse, and against his army. (Revelation 19:19)

And the beast was taken, and with him the false prophet that wrought miracles before him, with which he deceived them that had received the mark of the beast, and them that worshipped his image. These both were cast alive into a lake of fire burning with brimstone. (Revelation 19:20)

Once the Beast is introduced in Revelation chapter 11, he is constantly in the middle of the action until he is thrown into the lake of fire in Revelation chapter 19.

But before Revelation chapter 11, there is no mention of him at all.

In fact, we are repeatedly told in the Book of Revelation that the Beast ascends out of the pit, and that simply does not happen until Revelation chapter 11.

So anyone that is watching for the Antichrist to appear is going to have to wait three and a half years after the 7 year apocalypse has already started for that to happen.

I know that this may be confusing for many of you, and that is one reason why I am quoting so extensively from the Scriptures.

Just because you have been taught something in the past does not mean that it is accurate.

What matters is what the Scriptures actually say, and the Scriptures are very, very clear on this matter.

Even though the Antichrist does not come on the scene until the middle of the 7 year apocalypse, there are other signs that we can be watching for that will let us know with absolute certainty that the Tribulation period has begun.

This is what I will be talking about in the next chapter, so don't stop reading now...

3 SIGNS

In the last chapter, I discussed two things that many Christians believe will mark the beginning of the Great Tribulation. Unfortunately, they are watching for the wrong signs. As I explained, there will be no "7 year peace treaty" with Israel, and the Antichrist is not even going to come on the scene until halfway through the 7 year apocalypse.

So if those signs do not apply, how can we know that the 7 year apocalypse has actually begun?

Thankfully, the Scriptures do give us some specific things to watch for. The first is God's confirmation of His Covenant with Israel that we read about in Daniel 9:27. As I detailed in the last chapter, a translation of Daniel 9:27 that would be true to the original language would look something like this...

"The Covenant will be confirmed (or strengthened) with many for one week".

As I have already discussed, the Hebrew word for "Covenant" in Daniel 9:27 is the exact same Hebrew word that was used for God's Covenant with His people earlier in Daniel chapter 9.

So what will it look like when God confirms His Covenant with Israel at the start of the 7 year apocalypse?

At this point we don't know for sure, but Michael Rood and other scholars believe that it will have something to do with the Ark of the Covenant, and I am inclined to concur with that analysis.

The Ark of the Covenant was always the centerpiece of God's Covenant with Israel, and it is a direct link back to the period of history when God originally established that Covenant on Mt. Sinai. If the Ark still exists, and it does, then the tablets of stone containing the Ten Commandments should still be with it.

Over the centuries, there has been a tremendous amount of speculation about the fate of the Ark of the Covenant once it disappeared from the pages of history. Many feared that it was lost for good, but that is not the case. Centuries ago, the Ark was hidden in a deep underground chamber under the city of Jerusalem, and all of the evidence indicates that it is still there today. If you are interested in examining the evidence that the Ark of the Covenant still exists, I would encourage you to visit arkdiscovery.com.

Authorities in Israel know where the Ark is located, but all attempts to go in and retrieve it have been futile because God is not allowing that to happen yet. According to reports that have been leaked out of Israel, several individuals were actually struck dead during one attempt to retrieve the Ark. Could it be possible that God is waiting for the beginning of the 7 year apocalypse before He finally allows the discovery of the Ark to be revealed to the general public?

We don't know, but I am watching for any news regarding the Ark very carefully.

Of course God could theoretically confirm His Covenant with Israel in a multitude of other ways. We don't know for certain that the confirming of the Covenant will involve the Ark, and so we need to continue to seek God for wisdom on this issue.

A second sign that will let us know that the 7 year apocalypse has begun is the beginning of the ministry of the Two Witnesses. We are told that the ministry of the Two Witnesses will last for 1,260 days, and that represents a period of almost three and a half years on our modern secular calendar. Once that period of time is over, the Beast will ascend out of the pit and kill them. In Revelation 11, we are told that the whole world will greatly rejoice when the Beast finally slaughters the Two Witnesses...

3 And I will give power unto my two witnesses, and they shall prophesy a thousand two hundred and threescore days, clothed in sackcloth.

4 These are the two olive trees, and the two candlesticks standing before the God of the earth.

5 And if any man will hurt them, fire proceedeth out of their mouth, and devoureth their enemies: and if any man will hurt them, he must in this manner be killed.

6 These have power to shut heaven, that it rain not in the days of their prophecy: and have power over waters to turn them to blood, and to smite the earth with all plagues, as often as they will.

7 And when they shall have finished their testimony, the beast that ascendeth out of the bottomless pit shall make war against them, and shall overcome them, and kill them.

8 And their dead bodies shall lie in the street of the great city, which spiritually is called Sodom and Egypt, where also our Lord was crucified.

9 And they of the people and kindreds and tongues and nations shall see their dead bodies three days and an half, and shall not suffer their dead bodies to be put in graves.

10 And they that dwell upon the earth shall rejoice over them, and make merry, and shall send gifts one to another; because these two prophets tormented them that dwelt on the earth.

11 And after three days and an half the spirit of life from God entered into them, and they stood upon their feet; and great fear fell upon them which saw them.

12 And they heard a great voice from heaven saying unto them, Come up hither. And they ascended up to heaven in a cloud; and their enemies beheld them.

13 And the same hour was there a great earthquake, and the tenth part of the city fell, and in the earthquake were slain of men seven thousand: and the remnant were affrighted, and gave glory to the God of heaven.

The Two Witnesses will be greatly, greatly hated by most of the population of the world.

In fact, the Bible says that people will actually give gifts to one another to celebrate the fact that they are dead.

So to most of the planet, the Two Witnesses will be "the bad guys", and the Antichrist will be "the good guy" for killing them.

Over the centuries, there has been a tremendous amount of speculation about the identity of the Two Witnesses. Some Bible prophecy experts believe that Enoch and Elijah will be the Two Witnesses, others believe that Moses and Elijah will be the Two Witnesses, and over time there have been many, many other theories that have been widely circulated as well.

The truth is that the Scriptures do not tell us who they will be, and so we don't know for sure.

Personally, I will be watching for their appearance in the city of Jerusalem, but we don't even know for certain that their ministry will start there.

We know that the ministry of the Two Witnesses will end in the Holy City because that is where the Antichrist kills them, but we should not assume that they will be in just one place the entire time. That may turn out to be true, but we should not jump to any conclusions that go beyond what the Scriptures tell us.

When the ministry of the Two Witnesses begins, it will not be covered by ABC, CBS, NBC, CNN and Fox News. But eventually when they start smiting the Earth with plagues and those that come against them keep dropping dead, reports about these two men will start spreading like wildfire.

Throughout history, God has always done big things during His appointed times, and so I expect the ministry of the Two Witnesses to begin and end during Biblical festivals. But I certainly cannot be dogmatic about that either, because the Scriptures do not say for sure that this will be the case.

But once the Two Witnesses are on the scene, that will tell us very clearly that the 7 year apocalypse has begun.

A third sign that will tell us that the 7 year apocalypse has started will be the breaking of the seals in Revelation chapter 6...

And I saw when the Lamb opened one of the seals, and I heard, as it were the noise of thunder, one of the four beasts saying, Come and see.

2 And I saw, and behold a white horse: and he that sat on him had a bow; and a crown was given unto him: and he went forth conquering, and to conquer.

3 And when he had opened the second seal, I heard the second beast say, Come and see.

4 And there went out another horse that was red: and power was given to him that sat thereon to take peace from the earth, and that they should kill one another: and there was given unto him a great sword.

5 And when he had opened the third seal, I heard the third beast say, Come and see. And I beheld, and lo a black horse; and he that sat on him had a pair of balances in his hand.

6 And I heard a voice in the midst of the four beasts say, A measure of wheat for a penny, and three measures of barley for a penny; and see thou hurt not the oil and the wine.

7 And when he had opened the fourth seal, I heard the voice of the fourth beast say, Come and see.

8 And I looked, and behold a pale horse: and his name that sat on him was Death, and Hell followed with him. And power was given unto them over the fourth part of the earth, to kill with sword, and with hunger, and with death, and with the beasts of the earth.

9 And when he had opened the fifth seal, I saw under the altar the souls of them that were slain for the word of God, and for the testimony which they held:

10 And they cried with a loud voice, saying, How long, O Lord, holy and true, dost thou not judge and avenge our blood on them that dwell on the earth?

11 And white robes were given unto every one of them; and it was said unto them, that they should rest yet for a little season, until their fellowservants also and their brethren, that should be killed as they were, should be fulfilled.

12 And I beheld when he had opened the sixth seal, and, lo, there was a great earthquake; and the sun became black as sackcloth of hair, and the moon became as blood;

13 And the stars of heaven fell unto the earth, even as a fig tree casteth her untimely figs, when she is shaken of a mighty wind.

14 And the heaven departed as a scroll when it is rolled together; and every mountain and island were moved out of their places.

15 And the kings of the earth, and the great men, and the rich men, and the chief captains, and the mighty men, and every bondman, and every free man, hid themselves in the dens and in the rocks of the mountains;

16 And said to the mountains and rocks, Fall on us, and hide us from the face of him that sitteth on the throne, and from the wrath of the Lamb:

17 For the great day of his wrath is come; and who shall be able to stand?

When the white horse rides, that will clearly tell us that the 7 year apocalypse has officially commenced.

But right now, the identity of the rider of the white horse remains a deeply shrouded mystery. As I detailed in the last chapter, it cannot be the Antichrist, because the Antichrist does not emerge out of the pit until the middle of the Tribulation period.

I have been praying for insight into the rider of the white horse, and I would encourage you to do the same. I believe that the Lord will answer our prayers, but for the moment there is still so much that is unknown about the white horse.

However, the riding of the red horse should be much easier to identify. I believe that the red horse will ride very quickly after the white horse, and it will be a time when peace is taken from the Earth.

Personally, I believe that this is when the wars that I discussed in *Lost Prophecies Of The Future Of America* will begin. But the U.S. will not be involved in a nuclear conflict right away. In fact, to me it sounds like John's description of the opening of the sixth seal sounds a whole lot like nuclear war.

Let me put it another way so that readers can understand clearly what I am trying to communicate.

At this point, I believe that the surprise nuclear attack on the United States will come toward the end of the first half of the 7 year apocalypse. But the "wars and rumors of wars" that Jesus warned us about will really start to crank into high gear once the red horse rides.

As I write this book, Russia is on the verge of war with Ukraine, China is threatening to invade Taiwan, and Israel and Iran have already been attacking one another covertly on a regular basis. We should be monitoring all of those situations very carefully.

Eventually, war will engulf nearly the entire planet, and it will be a truly, truly horrible time for our world.

Once all three of the signs that I have discussed in this chapter have occurred, nobody will be able to deny that we have entered the 7 year apocalypse. As millions upon millions of people realize what has happened, it will cause a tremendous amount of fear and panic, but it will also cause vast multitudes to turn to God.

When that time arrives, we need to be ready to jump into the harvest fields, because it will be an opportunity to win souls for the Kingdom like we have never seen before.

THE FIRST HALF OF THE 7 YEAR APOCALYPSE

Out of the entire duration of human history, the Bible spends an inordinate amount of time warning us about the events of the last seven years just before the return of Jesus Christ. The reason God did this was not to scare us. He wants us to have peace about what is coming, and He wants us to understand that He knew about all of these events in advance, that He is in control, and that He has a plan. They are going to be incredibly difficult years, but they can also be absolutely amazing years for believers if we are willing to fully embrace His purposes. Ultimately, there is a redemptive purpose to these 7 years, because they will be undeniable proof to the entire world that Jesus is about to come back. I believe that this is going to result in a great end times harvest of souls, and that is definitely something that I want to be involved in.

Most Bible prophecy teachers correctly portray the Great Tribulation as a truly horrific time for humanity, but many of them don't really emphasize the fact that the first half of the 7 year period will actually be very different from the second half of the 7 year period.

In general, the first half will clearly demonstrate how futile it is for humanity to try to run things without God in the picture, and the second half will clearly demonstrate the futility of the Antichrist's reign.

All throughout human history, there have been great blessings when people have chosen to do things God's way, and there have been great curses when people have chosen to reject God and do things their own way. These lessons will be greatly magnified during the 7 year apocalypse, and the events of this 7 year period will set the stage for the 1,000 year reign of Christ from Jerusalem.

In this chapter, we are going to focus on what will happen during the first three and a half years of the Tribulation period. In a later chapter, we will focus on the second three and a half years.

Revelation chapter 6 and the first portion of Matthew chapter 24 both give us a rough outline of the first half of the 7 year apocalypse. First, let's review what both of these passages have to say, and then I want to point out some of the remarkable parallels between them.

Here is what Matthew 24:4-14 says in the King James Version...

4 And Jesus answered and said unto them, Take heed that no man deceive you.

5 For many shall come in my name, saying, I am Christ; and shall deceive many.

6 And ye shall hear of wars and rumours of wars: see that ye be not troubled: for all these things must come to pass, but the end is not yet.

7 For nation shall rise against nation, and kingdom against kingdom: and there shall be famines, and pestilences, and earthquakes, in divers places.

8 All these are the beginning of sorrows.

9 Then shall they deliver you up to be afflicted, and shall kill you:

and ye shall be hated of all nations for my name's sake.

10 And then shall many be offended, and shall betray one another, and shall hate one another.

11 And many false prophets shall rise, and shall deceive many.

12 And because iniquity shall abound, the love of many shall wax cold.

13 But he that shall endure unto the end, the same shall be saved.

14 And this gospel of the kingdom shall be preached in all the world for a witness unto all nations; and then shall the end come.

And here is what Revelation 6 says in the King James Version...

1 And I saw when the Lamb opened one of the seals, and I heard, as it were the noise of thunder, one of the four beasts saying, Come and see.

2 And I saw, and behold a white horse: and he that sat on him had a bow; and a crown was given unto him: and he went forth conquering, and to conquer.

3 And when he had opened the second seal, I heard the second beast say, Come and see.

4 And there went out another horse that was red: and power was given to him that sat thereon to take peace from the earth, and that they should kill one another: and there was given unto him a great sword.

5 And when he had opened the third seal, I heard the third beast say, Come and see. And I beheld, and lo a black horse; and he that sat on him had a pair of balances in his hand.

6 And I heard a voice in the midst of the four beasts say, A measure of wheat for a penny, and three measures of barley for a penny; and see thou hurt not the oil and the wine.

7 And when he had opened the fourth seal, I heard the voice of the fourth beast say, Come and see.

8 And I looked, and behold a pale horse: and his name that sat on him was Death, and Hell followed with him. And power was given unto them over the fourth part of the earth, to kill with sword, and with hunger, and with death, and with the beasts of the earth.

9 And when he had opened the fifth seal, I saw under the altar the souls of them that were slain for the word of God, and for the testimony which they held:

10 And they cried with a loud voice, saying, How long, O Lord, holy and true, dost thou not judge and avenge our blood on them that dwell on the earth?

11 And white robes were given unto every one of them; and it was said unto them, that they should rest yet for a little season, until their fellow servants also and their brethren, that should be killed as they were, should be fulfilled.

12 And I beheld when he had opened the sixth seal, and, lo, there was a great earthquake; and the sun became black as sackcloth of hair, and the moon became as blood;

13 And the stars of heaven fell unto the earth, even as a fig tree casteth her untimely figs, when she is shaken of a mighty wind.

14 And the heaven departed as a scroll when it is rolled together; and every mountain and island were moved out of their places.

15 And the kings of the earth, and the great men, and the rich men, and the chief captains, and the mighty men, and every bondman, and every free man, hid themselves in the dens and in the rocks of the mountains;

16 And said to the mountains and rocks, Fall on us, and hide us from the face of him that sitteth on the throne, and from the wrath of the Lamb:

17 For the great day of his wrath is come; and who shall be able to stand?

The first parallel that I would like for you to notice is that both passages speak of war. In Matthew 24, Jesus uses the phrase "wars and rumours of wars", and I think that "rumours of wars" accurately describes the current state of affairs. As I write this book, the conflict between Russia and Ukraine threatens to spark a global war, China is threatening military conflict if Taiwan declares independence, and Iran and Israel could start firing missiles at each other at any moment. Any of those conflicts would likely end up involving the United States, and by the time many of you read this book a major war may have already erupted.

In Revelation 6, the red horse rides once the second seal is opened. This would seem to imply that war will erupt very early during the first half of the 7 year Tribulation period. In verse 8, it tells us that a fourth part of the global population will end up dying during this time, and it lists the "sword" as one of the factors that will cause this mass carnage.

The population of the world is rapidly approaching the 8 billion mark, and so we are talking about the deaths of nearly 2 billion people.

We have never seen anything like this in all of human history, and it will be truly, truly horrifying.

The next parallel that I would like for you to notice is that both passages speak of famine. In Matthew 24, Jesus tells us that there will be "famines", and that would seem to indicate more than one. Just recently, World Food Program Executive Director David Beasley warned that our planet would soon be facing "famines of biblical proportions", and that should chill us to the core. The World Food Program is run by the United Nations, and David Beasley is a secular leader. When I first learned that he had used the phrase "famines of biblical proportions" it immediately got my attention. If the head of a UN agency is sounding the alarm about unprecedented global hunger, why aren't more churches talking about this?

In Revelation 6, verses five and six seem to indicate that a dramatic rise in food prices will precede the horrible global famines that are coming, and we are already starting to see food prices rise aggressively right now.

Then in verse 8, we are told that "hunger" will be one of the factors that kills a fourth part of the world population. In my last book, *Lost Prophecies Of The Future America*, I shared what numerous prophetic voices have been shown regarding the great famines that are coming. For years I have been strongly urging my readers to store up food so that they will be at least somewhat prepared for those times, but of course most people in the general population are not interested in listening to such warnings.

The third parallel that I would like for you to notice is that both passages appear to speak of pestilence. In Matthew 24, the word "pestilences" is used, and that would seem to imply multiple pandemics in the last days. We have already been dealing with the COVID pandemic, but as I discussed in my last book, I believe that the pandemics that are coming in the future will be much,

much worse.

If you believe the official numbers, COVID has killed millions, but I believe that the pandemics that are ahead will kill tens of millions.

In the King James Version, Revelation 6:8 lists "death" as one of the factors that will kill a fourth part of the global population during this time, but other translations use the word "plague" there. Of course sometimes those two terms are used inter-changeably. For example, the great pandemic that swept through Europe during the Middle Ages is known as "the Black Death", but it is also sometimes referred to as "the Black Plague".

As horrible as the COVID pandemic has been, I believe that what is coming during the first half of the 7 year apocalypse will make what we have gone through so far seem like a Sunday picnic.

The fourth parallel that I would like for you to notice is that both passages speak of seismic activity. In Matthew 24, Jesus speaks of earthquakes "in divers places", and in recent months we have definitely seen quite a bit of shaking. The number of large earth-quakes that we have seen so far this year is way above the num-ber that we saw last year, and once dormant volcanoes have been erupting all over the globe.

But eventually the seismic activity around the world will get much, much worse.

In Revelation 6:12-14, we are told about "a great earthquake" that will cause "every mountain and island" to be "moved out of their places".

That is quite an earthquake!

Others have pointed out that this particular passage may be describing an exchange of nuclear missiles. Verse 13 speaks of "the stars of heaven" falling to Earth, verse 14 says that heaven "departed as a scroll when it is rolled together", and verse 15 tells us of important men hiding themselves in the mountains.

Could it be possible that the Apostle John was trying to describe a nuclear war in the parlance of his day?

I don't know if we can be too dogmatic about that, but in my last book I detailed the fact that many prophetic voices have been shown that a great nuclear conflict is coming in the last days.

The fourth parallel that I would like for you to notice is that both passages speak of great persecution. In Matthew 24, two entire verses are used to describe the horrific persecution that is coming during this time...

9 Then shall they deliver you up to be afflicted, and shall kill you: and ye shall be hated of all nations for my name's sake.

10 And then shall many be offended, and shall betray one another, and shall hate one another.

In Revelation 6, those that have already been killed for their faith are told to be patient because this is a time when more of their "fellow servants" will be martyred just as they were.

These two passages seem to indicate that there will be great persecution even before the Antichrist arrives on the scene.

As I detail elsewhere in this book, the Antichrist does not appear until halfway through the seven year Tribulation period. He is "the beast that ascendeth out of the bottomless pit", and he is not released until the bottomless pit is opened in Revelation 9.

I know that this is counter to what is traditionally taught by most end times teachers, but nowhere in the Scriptures do we find the Antichrist doing anything before the second half of the Tribulation period. The main passage where people get the idea that the Antichrist shows up at the beginning of the 7 year Tribulation period is Daniel 9, and I deal with that controversy in another chapter in this book.

But there will be tremendous persecution of believers even before the Antichrist arrives on the scene, and all of us need to be prepared for that.

The good news is that it will also be a time when God is moving in amazing ways.

In Matthew 24:14, we are told that "this gospel of the kingdom shall be preached in all the world for a witness unto all nations; and then shall the end come".

I believe that this will be the generation that finally fulfills the Great Commission, and I believe that we are on the verge of the greatest harvest of souls the world has ever seen.

In every believer, God has placed a hunger to do good and to make a difference. For some of us, that hunger may have been deeply buried by years of hurt, pain and frustration, but it is still there.

No matter what you have been through in the past, God can still greatly use you if you are willing to repent and turn back to Him.

God has placed you at this particular moment in history for a reason. All of human history has been building up to a grand crescendo, and we are fortunate enough to be here for it.

So don't listen to those that are telling you that your life will never amount to anything. You were born for such a time as this, and God has a plan for you.

But you have got to be willing to surrender everything to Him.

The greatest thing that you can do for someone else is to lead that individual to faith in Jesus Christ. Those that are born again have eternal life, and that is a gift of infinite value.

When you stand before God, what are you going to have to show for your life?

Perhaps many of you would not have a good answer to that question right now, but that can change.

The years ahead are going to be exceptionally challenging, but they will also be times when new heroes are forged.

No matter what the rest of your life has looked like, you can still be involved in the great end times army that God is now raising up.

But you have to be totally committed, because God doesn't want anything less from us.

I believe that this end times army is going to lead millions upon millions of people into the Kingdom, and you can be part of that.

During the times of the early church, it is estimated that the total global population was somewhere around 200 million.

Today, there are more than 7 billion people living on our planet.

That means that there is 35 times as many souls to be won, and we now possess technology that allows us to instantly reach people on the other side of the globe with our message.

What an exciting time to be alive!

If you have made your life all about your bank account, your house, your possessions, your stock market portfolio and your career plans, you are going to be absolutely shattered by the times that are coming.

But if you surrender absolutely everything to Christ and live for Him and for His Kingdom, the times ahead can be greater than you ever dreamed possible.

We need to stop focusing on the things that are just temporary, and we need to start fixing our eyes on the things that are eternal.

The things of this world are passing away, but the things that are eternal will last forever.

WORMWOOD

After the seven seals have been opened, but before the Beast rises out of the pit at the sounding of the fifth trumpet, the sounding of the first four trumpets will set in motion a series of events that will collectively represent the worst cataclysm that the world has seen since the days of Noah's flood. Vast numbers of people that have been fortunate enough to survive the horrors unleashed by the opening of the seven seals will perish during this time, and this unprecedented disaster will set the stage for the coming of the Antichrist.

In the last chapter, I dealt with the opening of the seals during the first half of the 7 year apocalypse, and in the next chapter I will dig into the appearance of the Beast and the events of the second half of the 7 year apocalypse.

I wanted to deal with the blowing of the first four trumpets in a completely separate chapter, because there is a lot of debate about the exact timing of these events. Some believe that the blowing of the first trumpet marks the midpoint of the Tribulation period. Others believe that it comes very early during the second half of the Tribulation.

Personally, I believe that the blowing of the first four trumpets happens near the end of the first half of the 7 year apocalypse. As I discuss elsewhere in this book, we know that the Antichrist is given three and a half years to do his thing, and we also know that the abomination of desolation takes place in the middle of the 7 year period.

Since the events of the first four trumpets take place before the Antichrist rises and goes to Jerusalem to commit the abomination of desolation, I place the first four trumpets prior to the midpoint of the Tribulation on my timeline.

But no matter what your perspective is, most Bible prophecy teachers agree that we are talking about events that happen somewhere around the middle of the seven years.

We read about the blowing of the first four trumpets in Revelation chapter 8. As I read these verses, I get the impression that these events happen in rapid fire fashion and that they are all part of a single overall cataclysmic event...

And when he had opened the seventh seal, there was silence in heaven about the space of half an hour.

2 And I saw the seven angels which stood before God; and to them were given seven trumpets.

3 And another angel came and stood at the altar, having a golden censer; and there was given unto him much incense, that he should offer it with the prayers of all saints upon the golden altar which was before the throne.

4 And the smoke of the incense, which came with the prayers of the saints, ascended up before God out of the angel's hand.

5 And the angel took the censer, and filled it with fire of the altar, and cast it into the earth: and there were voices, and thunderings, and lightnings, and an earthquake.

6 And the seven angels which had the seven trumpets prepared themselves to sound.

7 The first angel sounded, and there followed hail and fire mingled with blood, and they were cast upon the earth: and the third part of trees was burnt up, and all green grass was burnt up.

8 And the second angel sounded, and as it were a great mountain burning with fire was cast into the sea: and the third part of the sea became blood;

9 And the third part of the creatures which were in the sea, and had life, died; and the third part of the ships were destroyed.

10 And the third angel sounded, and there fell a great star from heaven, burning as it were a lamp, and it fell upon the third part of the rivers, and upon the fountains of waters;

11 And the name of the star is called Wormwood: and the third part of the waters became wormwood; and many men died of the waters, because they were made bitter.

12 And the fourth angel sounded, and the third part of the sun was smitten, and the third part of the moon, and the third part of the stars; so as the third part of them was darkened, and the day shone not for a third part of it, and the night likewise.

13 And I beheld, and heard an angel flying through the midst of heaven, saying with a loud voice, Woe, woe, woe, to the inhabiters of the earth by reason of the other voices of the trumpet of the three angels, which are yet to sound!

Let's take each trumpet one at a time.

Once the first trumpet is blown, it appears that the Earth enters some sort of a debris field. Verse 7 reminds me of Hollywood disaster movies that I have seen in which our planet is suddenly pelted by large numbers of small asteroids. If lots and lots of flaming space rocks hit the Earth's surface in a very short period of time, that would definitely cause a lot of very large fires.

But the devastation described here is difficult for me to wrap my head around. We are told that trees and grass are burned up on a massive scale, and even as I write this I am having a difficult time imagining what that would look like.

And once so much vegetation has been burned, that would just make the ongoing global famines a whole lot worse.

On the heels of the first trumpet, a massive asteroid appears to hit our planet as the result of the blowing of the second trumpet.

In my last book, I shared a large number of prophecies from men and women of God that have been shown that someday a giant asteroid will strike the Atlantic Ocean with great violence. This will create a tsunami that is hundreds of feet high which will slam into cities along the east coast of the United States and other coastal cities around the globe with incredible force. If you have ever seen the tsunami scene in the movie *Deep Impact*, that will give you some idea of what I am talking about.

This colossal tsunami will make the tsunami that hit Fukushima a number of years ago look absolutely pathetic in comparison. Some prophetic voices have been shown that the wall of water will actually make it all the way to the Appalachian mountains. Countless major cities will be instantly eliminated from the map and hundreds of millions of people around the world will die.

I believe that Revelation 8 describes this event. In verse 8 we are told that a "great mountain burning with fire" plunges into the sea. That is a perfect description of what a huge asteroid would look like as it hits the Atlantic Ocean. If we could see it happen, we would see a giant pile of rock that is spectacularly burning as it plunges through our atmosphere toward the ocean.

Right after that happens, the third angel sounds his trumpet.

Pastor Paul Begley has pointed out that it appears that another very large asteroid hits our planet once this third trumpet is blown. Just when it seems as though things can't possibly get any worse, that is precisely what happens.

In verses 10 and 11, the word that is translated as "star" in the King James Version is actually the Greek word "aster" from which our word "asteroid" is derived. The Apostle John was doing his best to describe what he was being shown in the language of his day, and I think that he did a really great job.

This second asteroid appears to hit land, and the impact will apparently result in much of the fresh water around the planet becoming unsuitable for drinking.

Needless to say, two major asteroid impacts will throw enormous amounts of dust and debris up into our atmosphere. Much of that dust and debris will hang in the atmosphere for some time, and that could account for the darkness that happens once the fourth angel blows his trumpet.

I don't know if I even have the words to appropriately describe the death and devastation that will happen during this time. It will be unlike anything that we have ever seen before in all of human history, and the death toll will be off the charts.

It is in such an environment that the fifth trumpet will sound and the Antichrist will rise for his three and a half year reign.

Just think about it. The "Wormwood event" will cap off three and a half years of wars, disasters and other nightmarish events, and humanity will be at the lowest point ever.

It is at this moment that the Antichrist will appear on the scene as "humanity's savior", and vast multitudes will welcome him with open arms.

You may still be alive at that point, but first you will have to survive everything that is going to happen up to that time.

If you are able to make it through the opening of the seven seals, you will want to get as far away from any coasts that border the Atlantic Ocean as you possibly can. Once the asteroid strikes, there will be nowhere to run and nowhere to hide. If you are living in a coastal community at that point, there is a very good chance that you will die unless God intervenes with some sort of a supernatural miracle.

I know that I am being quite blunt. Unfortunately, the vast majority of our churches are not even talking about these things, and believers need watchmen that will tell it to them straight.

Before I end this chapter, there is something else that I should address. There has been a tremendous amount of speculation that an asteroid known as Apophis will hit our planet on April 13th, 2029. This has led many to suggest that Apophis is Wormwood and that the Tribulation period will begin during the second half of 2025.

After carefully investigating the matter, I do not believe that any of this is accurate.

For one thing, there is no debris field accompanying Apophis, and Apophis is not big enough by itself to cause all of the damage described in Revelation 8.

In addition, the orbit of Apophis is now very well known, and on their official website NASA officials are assuring us that "there is no risk of Apophis impacting our planet for at least a century". Of course it is always possible that NASA could be lying, because NASA has not always been honest with us in the past.

But scientific authorities all over the globe have all come to the exact same conclusion. Are all of those scientists around the world all involved in some grand conspiracy to deceive the public?

That is theoretically possible, but the evidence that I have seen seems quite persuasive. I do not believe that Apophis will even come close to hitting us.

But that certainly does not mean that we are safe for the foreseeable future.

In fact, giant asteroids could potentially slam into our planet long before 2029 rolls around.

We live at a time when the number of near-Earth objects that are whizzing past our planet is dramatically increasing. Many of them we do not discover until they are just days away, and there are others that we never even see until they have already gone past our planet.

So those that believe that our scientists have a really good idea of what is going on up there are just dead wrong. The truth is that our ability to detect incoming space rocks is still very limited.

There is a very good chance that our scientists have not discovered the asteroids that are described in Revelation 8 yet, and it is also possible that they may not even exist at this point. At some point in the future, God could supernaturally create new asteroids and release them toward our planet at just the right time.

We just don't know.

God is God, and He can do things however He desires.

But Revelation 8 does make it clear that a tremendous cataclysm is coming. God told the Apostle John that it is coming, and there is no changing that.

Once the 7 year apocalypse officially starts, the countdown to that cataclysm will begin.

I will be sounding the alarm as loudly as I can, but I sure wish that a lot more voices were doing the same thing.

THE SECOND HALF OF
THE 7 YEAR APOCALYPSE

As I have discussed previously, the first half of the 7 year apocalypse is going to be far different from the second half of the 7 year apocalypse. During the first half, we are going to see the final outcome of humanity's attempts to run the planet. There will be wars, pestilences, great economic troubles and widespread famines. It will turn out to be a complete and total horror show, but before Jesus comes back and sets everything right, someone else is going to come along and try to run things.

The Antichrist is actually going to be an imposter. When he arises at the midpoint of the 7 year apocalypse, most of the world will welcome him as a conquering hero. He will be hailed as a "messiah", but he won't be anything like the Lord Jesus Christ. In fact, this false messiah will relentlessly hunt true Christians down and brutally slaughter them.

In this chapter, we are going to look at three passages of Scripture that specifically address the second half of the 7 year apocalypse. I will be quoting large blocks of text from these passages because it is so important to see things in context. So many Bible teachers pull out a verse here and a verse there and attempt to make up entire doctrines out of nothing. The Bible is actually very clear about most things, and it is always critical to read everything in context.

The first passage that I would like for us to examine is Matthew 24:15-31...

15 When ye therefore shall see the abomination of desolation, spoken of by Daniel the prophet, stand in the holy place, (whoso readeth, let him understand:)

16 Then let them which be in Judaea flee into the mountains:

17 Let him which is on the housetop not come down to take any thing out of his house:

18 Neither let him which is in the field return back to take his clothes.

19 And woe unto them that are with child, and to them that give suck in those days!

20 But pray ye that your flight be not in the winter, neither on the sabbath day:

21 For then shall be great tribulation, such as was not since the beginning of the world to this time, no, nor ever shall be.

22 And except those days should be shortened, there should no flesh be saved: but for the elect's sake those days shall be shortened.

23 Then if any man shall say unto you, Lo, here is Christ, or there; believe it not.

24 For there shall arise false Christs, and false prophets, and shall shew great signs and wonders; insomuch that, if it were possible, they shall deceive the very elect.

25 Behold, I have told you before.

26 Wherefore if they shall say unto you, Behold, he is in the desert; go not forth: behold, he is in the secret chambers; believe it not.

27 For as the lightning cometh out of the east, and shineth even unto the west; so shall also the coming of the Son of man be.

28 For wheresoever the carcase is, there will the eagles be gathered together.

29 Immediately after the tribulation of those days shall the sun be darkened, and the moon shall not give her light, and the stars shall fall from heaven, and the powers of the heavens shall be shaken:

30 And then shall appear the sign of the Son of man in heaven: and then shall all the tribes of the earth mourn, and they shall see the Son of man coming in the clouds of heaven with power and great glory.

31 And he shall send his angels with a great sound of a trumpet, and they shall gather together his elect from the four winds, from one end of heaven to the other.

From Daniel 9, we know that the abomination of desolation marks the midpoint of the 7 year apocalypse. If you are a veteran student of Bible prophecy, this concept will not be new to you.

Once the abomination of desolation happens, Jesus instructs those that are living in the region to flee to the mountains. Jesus tells believers to flee because from that point forward the Antichrist is going to be conducting an all-out war against Christians.

In Revelation 12, we read that there is a specific place of protection that God has prepared in the wilderness where believers will be sheltered for a three and a half year period. There has been a tremendous amount of speculation about the exact location of that place of protection in the mountains, and this is something that is of great interest to me personally, but I will not add to that speculation here.

When the time comes for believers in the land of Israel to flee to the mountains, I believe that God will give very specific directions about where to go. So don't be too stressed out if it remains a mystery for now.

I have been asked if there will be other places of protection other than the one mentioned in the Book of Revelation, and I think that is a legitimate question.

We are not told that there will be, and we are not told that there will not be.

God could certainly choose to supernaturally protect His people in any manner that He sees fit. But as we will see in Revelation 13 below, this is also a period of time when the Antichrist is granted power to make war against the saints. So that would seem to imply that in most areas of the globe saints are not being supernaturally protected during this time.

So I would say that the only guarantee of safety during this time is to be in the specific place of protection that Jesus talks about in Matthew 24.

A lot of Bible prophecy teachers tend to assume that the Antichrist will be some politician or prominent individual that is roaming the planet today, but the Bible makes it clear that he comes from somewhere else. He actually arises out of the bottomless pit, and we read about this in Revelation 9...

And the fifth angel sounded, and I saw a star fall from heaven unto the earth: and to him was given the key of the bottomless pit.

2 And he opened the bottomless pit; and there arose a smoke out of the pit, as the smoke of a great furnace; and the sun and the air were darkened by reason of the smoke of the pit.

3 And there came out of the smoke locusts upon the earth: and unto them was given power, as the scorpions of the earth have power.

4 And it was commanded them that they should not hurt the grass of the earth, neither any green thing, neither any tree; but only those men which have not the seal of God in their foreheads.

5 And to them it was given that they should not kill them, but that they should be tormented five months: and their torment was as the torment of a scorpion, when he striketh a man.

6 And in those days shall men seek death, and shall not find it; and shall desire to die, and death shall flee from them.

7 And the shapes of the locusts were like unto horses prepared unto battle; and on their heads were as it were crowns like gold, and their faces were as the faces of men.

8 And they had hair as the hair of women, and their teeth were as the teeth of lions.

9 And they had breastplates, as it were breastplates of iron; and the sound of their wings was as the sound of chariots of many horses running to battle.

10 And they had tails like unto scorpions, and there were stings in their tails: and their power was to hurt men five months.

11 And they had a king over them, which is the angel of the bottomless pit, whose name in the Hebrew tongue is Abaddon, but in the Greek tongue hath his name Apollyon.

12 One woe is past; and, behold, there come two woes more hereafter.

13 And the sixth angel sounded, and I heard a voice from the four horns of the golden altar which is before God,

14 Saying to the sixth angel which had the trumpet, Loose the four angels which are bound in the great river Euphrates.

15 And the four angels were loosed, which were prepared for an hour, and a day, and a month, and a year, for to slay the third part of men.

16 And the number of the army of the horsemen were two hundred thousand thousand: and I heard the number of them.

17 And thus I saw the horses in the vision, and them that sat on them, having breastplates of fire, and of jacinth, and brimstone: and the heads of the horses were as the heads of lions; and out of their mouths issued fire and smoke and brimstone.

18 By these three was the third part of men killed, by the fire, and by the smoke, and by the brimstone, which issued out of their mouths.

19 For their power is in their mouth, and in their tails: for their tails were like unto serpents, and had heads, and with them they do hurt.

20 And the rest of the men which were not killed by these plagues yet repented not of the works of their hands, that they should not worship devils, and idols of gold, and silver, and brass, and stone, and of wood: which neither can see, nor hear, nor walk:

21 Neither repented they of their murders, nor of their sorceries, nor of their fornication, nor of their thefts.

The more I read this chapter, the more it sounds like something out of a science fiction movie.

Over the decades, so many Bible prophecy teachers have deeply struggled to explain the events of the fifth and sixth trumpets, and that is because they fundamentally misunderstand what is happening here.

What is described in Revelation chapter 9 is literally an invasion of Earth by supernatural forces from the bottomless pit. It will make any "alien invasion" movie that Hollywood has ever dreamed up look extremely tame by comparison.

The Antichrist will attempt to convince everyone that he is arriving as "the conquering messiah" with the "armies of heaven" accompanying him, but true believers will see right through his charade.

Initially, many may attempt to fight back against the Antichrist and his supernatural armies, but they won't stand a chance. In fact, verse 15 says that a third part of the entire population of the globe will be wiped out during this time.

To call that a bloodbath would be a massive understatement.

Once he has crushed all opposition, the Antichrist will literally rule the world with an iron fist, and Revelation 13 gives us quite a few details about what life will be like under this new regime...

And I stood upon the sand of the sea, and saw a beast rise up out of the sea, having seven heads and ten horns, and upon his horns ten crowns, and upon his heads the name of blasphemy.

2 And the beast which I saw was like unto a leopard, and his feet were as the feet of a bear, and his mouth as the mouth of a lion: and the dragon gave him his power, and his seat, and great authority.

3 And I saw one of his heads as it were wounded to death; and his deadly wound was healed: and all the world wondered after the beast.

4 And they worshipped the dragon which gave power unto the beast: and they worshipped the beast, saying, Who is like unto the beast?

who is able to make war with him?

5 And there was given unto him a mouth speaking great things and blasphemies; and power was given unto him to continue forty and two months.

6 And he opened his mouth in blasphemy against God, to blaspheme his name, and his tabernacle, and them that dwell in heaven.

7 And it was given unto him to make war with the saints, and to overcome them: and power was given him over all kindreds, and tongues, and nations.

8 And all that dwell upon the earth shall worship him, whose names are not written in the book of life of the Lamb slain from the foundation of the world.

9 If any man have an ear, let him hear.

10 He that leadeth into captivity shall go into captivity: he that killeth with the sword must be killed with the sword. Here is the patience and the faith of the saints.

11 And I beheld another beast coming up out of the earth; and he had two horns like a lamb, and he spake as a dragon.

12 And he exerciseth all the power of the first beast before him, and causeth the earth and them which dwell therein to worship the first beast, whose deadly wound was healed.

13 And he doeth great wonders, so that he maketh fire come down from heaven on the earth in the sight of men,

14 And deceiveth them that dwell on the earth by the means of those miracles which he had power to do in the sight of the beast; saying to them that dwell on the earth, that they should make an image to the

65

beast, which had the wound by a sword, and did live.

15 And he had power to give life unto the image of the beast, that the image of the beast should both speak, and cause that as many as would not worship the image of the beast should be killed.

16 And he causeth all, both small and great, rich and poor, free and bond, to receive a mark in their right hand, or in their foreheads:

17 And that no man might buy or sell, save he that had the mark, or the name of the beast, or the number of his name.

18 Here is wisdom. Let him that hath understanding count the number of the beast: for it is the number of a man; and his number is Six hundred threescore and six.

Once again, I want to point out the 42 month time period mentioned in verse 5.

All my life I was taught that the Antichrist would be on the scene for 7 years. But over and over again, the Scriptures make it clear that it will just be for three and a half years.

Of course those three and a half years will seem like they are lasting forever for those that are still alive at that time.

We are also told that a false prophet will arise as well, and this false prophet will essentially be the head of a new one world religion that worships the Antichrist. Adherents of various major global religions that make it through the Antichrist's initial slaughter will embrace him as "messiah", and verse 8 tells us that "all that dwell upon the earth shall worship him" except for true Bible-believing Christians.

It is in this environment that the "Mark of the Beast" will be introduced.

If you refuse the Mark of the Beast, things will not go well for you. In fact, Revelation 20:4 seems to imply that many of those that refuse to take the Mark of the Beast will be beheaded for making that choice.

But if you do take the Mark of the Beast, there is no hope for your soul. We find the following three verses in Revelation 14...

9 And the third angel followed them, saying with a loud voice, If any man worship the beast and his image, and receive his mark in his forehead, or in his hand,

10 The same shall drink of the wine of the wrath of God, which is poured out without mixture into the cup of his indignation; and he shall be tormented with fire and brimstone in the presence of the holy angels, and in the presence of the Lamb:

11 And the smoke of their torment ascendeth up for ever and ever: and they have no rest day nor night, who worship the beast and his image, and whosoever receiveth the mark of his name.

Once we get to this point, there will be no middle ground.

Either you will follow Christ, or you will follow Antichrist.

Right now, churches all over the world need to be preparing their people to face the persecution that is ahead. Sadly, most churches in the western world don't ever talk about these things, and instead many of them are preaching a "prosperity gospel" that isn't going to end up doing anyone any good.

Quite a few books and movies have attempted to portray the Antichrist as a bumbling idiot, but that is not going to be the case at all.

The Antichrist will be a man with some sort of mysterious link to humanity's past, but he will also be a demonically-infused super creature capable of killing the Two Witnesses, successfully making war against the saints, and wiping out a third of the global population with his supernatural armies.

The only one able to defeat the Antichrist will be Jesus, and that will take place once the 7 year apocalypse has concluded.

I know that many of the things that I have shared with you in this chapter are difficult to digest, but God would not have placed you at this time in human history if you could not handle them.

In the years ahead, it will be so imperative for us to have the perspective that our lives are not our own.

If we live, we do so for Christ.

And if we die, we do so for Christ as well.

Any pain or suffering in this life are temporary, but any rewards for what we do in this life are eternal.

If you are living this life only for yourself, and if you are absolutely determined to cling to this life with all your might, then you will be highly vulnerable when the time of the Mark of the Beast finally arrives.

Once you take the Mark of the Beast, there is no more hope for you ever.

I cannot say that strongly enough.

There is no turning back once you have received the Mark of the Beast, and that is a message that we need to boldly proclaim to as many people as possible before we ever get to that point.

Because ultimately we are in a battle for souls, and every single precious soul that we can pull away from the clutches of darkness is a colossal victory for the Kingdom.

I will have so much more to say about all of this in the years ahead, but in this book I am just trying to give everyone a broad overview of what is coming.

Yes, I know that these things are scary. But God is in control, and He will be our Rock no matter what comes our way.

THE SECOND COMING

Many have a sense of dread as they read about the events of the 7 year apocalypse described in the Bible, but those of us that are believers should have a very different perspective. As the end times prophecies in the Bible are fulfilled, we should be filled with joy because it means that the return of our Lord and Savior is drawing near. Our destiny is to live with Him in His Kingdom forever, and that means that wherever you are living now is not your home. Our home is with Jesus, and we must never forget that.

Once the 7 year apocalypse has begun, we will officially be able to count down the days until we finally see our Messiah. Yes, the short-term circumstances will be exceedingly challenging, but if our eyes are fixed on Jesus we will be able to deal with whatever comes with joy because we know the end of the story.

The second coming of Jesus happens immediately after the 7 year apocalypse ends. At the last trumpet, believers all over the globe are caught up to meet the Lord in the air, and we are taken to heaven to celebrate the wedding supper of the Lamb. Meanwhile, the seven vials of God's wrath are poured out on the Earth to prepare the way for the most dramatic moment in human history. Revelation 19 tells us that Jesus will be riding a white horse as He leads His armies back to Earth to fight against the forces of Antichrist. A decisive battle results in the forces of Antichrist being completely defeated, Satan is bound for a thousand years, and Jesus sets up His Kingdom in Jerusalem. Following the Millennial reign, Satan is released one more time and there is one last major confrontation. Satan loses that confrontation, the remainder of humanity is judged, and God establishes a new heaven and a new Earth where we will live forever.

Unfortunately, a deeply flawed theory that has only become popular in the last couple hundred years has caused millions upon millions of believers in the western world to become very confused about the order of events. Today, it is commonly believed that Jesus will gather believers and take them to heaven before the 7 year apocalypse begins even though there is not a single verse in the Bible that says this is the case. In fact, the Bible makes it exceedingly clear that Jesus gathers believers to Himself once the Tribulation period has ended.

Those that believe in a "pre-Tribulation rapture" will acknowledge that a trumpet sounds and Christ's elect are gathered at the end of the Tribulation, but they also insist that there is another gathering at the beginning of the seven year period. So those that believe in a pre-Tribulation rapture actually believe in "multiple raptures" and "multiple resurrections". I know that sounds really absurd when it is put this way, but this is what they actually believe. They believe that the first rapture is for those that have been born again before the Tribulation begins, and they believe that the second rapture is for "Tribulation saints".

But the Bible leaves no room for debate. I wrote an entire book entitled *The Rapture Verdict* that proves that there is only one rapture and that it comes at the end of the 7 year apocalypse.

Throughout the New Testament, the Greek word "parousia" is repeatedly used to identify the Lord's return. Most of the time it is translated as "coming", but in two instances in the New Testament "parousia" is translated as "presence" in the King James Version.

In this chapter I am once again going to share large blocks of Scripture so that you can see everything in context. In the four examples that I have shared below, I have replaced the English word "coming" with the original Greek word "parousia" so that you can clearly see the point that I am trying to make.

Those that believe in a pre-Tribulation rapture carefully avoid using the term "resurrection", because the Bible clearly tells us that the resurrection of believers takes place at the "parousia" of Jesus. The following comes from 1 Corinthians 15...

20 But now is Christ risen from the dead, and become the firstfruits of them that slept.

21 For since by man came death, by man came also the resurrection of the dead.

22 For as in Adam all die, even so in Christ shall all be made alive.

23 But every man in his own order: Christ the firstfruits; afterward they that are Christ's at his parousia.

Could that be any clearer?

Christians that are now dead are resurrected or "raptured" at Christ's "parousia".

Nobody can deny that.

So precisely when is the "parousia"?

The disciples of Jesus asked Him this exact question in Matthew 24...

And Jesus went out, and departed from the temple: and his disciples came to him for to shew him the buildings of the temple.

2 And Jesus said unto them, See ye not all these things? verily I say unto you, There shall not be left here one stone upon another, that shall not be thrown down.

3 And as he sat upon the mount of Olives, the disciples came unto him privately, saying, Tell us, when shall these things be? and what shall be the sign of thy parousia, and of the end of the world?

From verse 4 through verse 26, Jesus goes on to describe events that will indicate that His return is imminent, and then in verse 27 He begins to address the specific timing of the "parousia"...

27 For as the lightning cometh out of the east, and shineth even unto the west; so shall also the parousia of the Son of man be.

28 For wheresoever the carcase is, there will the eagles be gathered together.

29 Immediately after the tribulation of those days shall the sun be darkened, and the moon shall not give her light, and the stars shall fall from heaven, and the powers of the heavens shall be shaken:

30 And then shall appear the sign of the Son of man in heaven: and then shall all the tribes of the earth mourn, and they shall see the Son of man coming in the clouds of heaven with power and great glory.

31 And he shall send his angels with a great sound of a trumpet, and they shall gather together his elect from the four winds, from one end of heaven to the other.

32 Now learn a parable of the fig tree; When his branch is yet tender, and putteth forth leaves, ye know that summer is nigh:

33 So likewise ye, when ye shall see all these things, know that it is near, even at the doors.

34 Verily I say unto you, This generation shall not pass, till all these things be fulfilled.

35 Heaven and earth shall pass away, but my words shall not pass away.

36 But of that day and hour knoweth no man, no, not the angels of heaven, but my Father only.

37 But as the days of Noah were, so shall also the parousia of the Son of man be.

38 For as in the days that were before the flood they were eating and drinking, marrying and giving in marriage, until the day that Noe entered into the ark,

39 And knew not until the flood came, and took them all away; so shall also the parousia of the Son of man be.

There you have it straight from the mouth of Jesus.

The "parousia" comes "immediately after the tribulation of those days". All of the things that Jesus described from verse 4 through verse 26 must happen first, and then the "parousia" will happen. A trumpet will sound, believers will be gathered from all over the globe, and we will finally be with Jesus forever.

In 1 Thessalonians 4, the Apostle Paul also tells us that the "parousia" will involve the sounding of a trumpet and the resurrection of dead believers...

14 For if we believe that Jesus died and rose again, even so them also which sleep in Jesus will God bring with him.

15 For this we say unto you by the word of the Lord, that we which are alive and remain unto the parousia of the Lord shall not prevent them which are asleep.

16 For the Lord himself shall descend from heaven with a shout, with the voice of the archangel, and with the trump of God: and the dead in Christ shall rise first:

17 Then we which are alive and remain shall be caught up together with them in the clouds, to meet the Lord in the air: and so shall we ever be with the Lord.

And in 2 Thessalonians 2, the Apostle Paul tells us that a series of events must happen before the "parousia" can take place. This includes the coming of the Antichrist...

Now we beseech you, brethren, by the parousia of our Lord Jesus Christ, and by our gathering together unto him,

2 That ye be not soon shaken in mind, or be troubled, neither by spirit, nor by word, nor by letter as from us, as that the day of Christ is at hand.

3 Let no man deceive you by any means: for that day shall not come, except there come a falling away first, and that man of sin be revealed, the son of perdition;

4 Who opposeth and exalteth himself above all that is called God, or that is worshipped; so that he as God sitteth in the temple of God, shewing himself that he is God.

5 Remember ye not, that, when I was yet with you, I told you these things?

6 And now ye know what withholdeth that he might be revealed in his time.

7 For the mystery of iniquity doth already work: only he who now letteth will let, until he be taken out of the way.

8 And then shall that Wicked be revealed, whom the Lord shall consume with the spirit of his mouth, and shall destroy with the brightness of his parousia:

As Revelation 19 explains, the Antichrist and his forces will be destroyed when Jesus returns, and 2 Thessalonians 2 specifically links that battle with the "parousia".

There should be absolutely no confusion among God's people about any of this. The Bible makes it super clear that the rapture happens at the "parousia" and that the "parousia" does not take place until the end of the 7 year apocalypse.

I could go on and on, but that is not the focus of this book. For much more on all of this, please see my previous book entitled *The Rapture Verdict.*

But even though the timing of the rapture is not the focus of this book, I knew that I had to address this issue because a lot of readers would be wondering why I seemed to be assuming that Christians would be here for the events of the Tribulation period.

All throughout the past 2,000 years, Christians have been brutally persecuted all over the globe. In our time, Christians have been tortured for months on end in secret facilities in China, ISIS terrorists have beheaded Christians in the Middle East, gunmen have regularly gone rampaging through Christian communities in various parts of Africa, and many believers in North Korea are shipped off to concentration camps and are never heard from again. But millions of believers in the western world are entirely convinced that we are a special group that will never have to go through any suffering.

This is a very dangerous delusion, because the vast majority of our churches are not preparing their people to face the brutal persecution that is eventually coming.

When the 7 year apocalypse begins and millions of Christians that had believed in a "pre-Tribulation rapture" realize that they are still here, many of them will plunge into a very deep state of depression.

But that should not happen. Yes, the years ahead will be extremely difficult, but God specifically placed you at this critical moment in human history for a reason.

God has specific jobs for each one of us to do, but if you are endlessly wallowing in a pit of despair you will never fulfill the destiny that He has for you.

What is the worst that could happen? Martyrs throughout Christian history have considered it to be a great honor to give their lives for their Savior. In the years ahead, countless believers will be faced with a choice of either renouncing their faith or laying down their lives for Jesus, and we need to be preparing the body of Christ for such moments.

As I have said before, God would not have put you at this point in history if He did not think that you could handle what is ahead.

Throughout the 7 year apocalypse, multitudes of believers will lay down their lives for Jesus, and they will bring great glory to God in the process.

And when it is all over, Jesus is going to come back and take us all home. We will live with Him forever and ever, and that is a prize that is far greater than anything that the world could possibly ever offer.

THE MILLENNIAL DAY THEORY

Throughout the centuries, prominent Christian leaders have expressed a belief that God has a 7,000 year plan for human history. In the Scriptures we are told that "one day is as a thousand years, and a thousand years as one day", and we know that the Millennial reign of Christ (also known as "the Day of the Lord") will last for 1,000 years. So if the Millennial reign corresponds to the Sabbath in the weekly cycle that God instituted at the very beginning, that should mean that there are six other "days" of 1,000 years each that precede the Millennial reign.

For those that are skeptical, please keep reading. Even though the Millennial Day theory is a minority position today, it was a very widely held view throughout most of the last 2,000 years. And if this position is true, that means that the 7 year apocalypse and the Millennial reign should be right around the corner.

It is imperative to remember that everything about the calendar that God set up at the very beginning of time is prophetic. Just like the festival days that God has instituted, the Sabbath is about looking back and remembering what God has done and it is also a prophecy about the future.

On the Sabbath, we remember that God created the world in six days and rested on the seventh day.

And on the Sabbath we also look forward to the "Day of the Lord" when Jesus will reign from Jerusalem and the world will finally be at peace.

In the next chapter, I am going to share a long list of early church leaders that believed this theory. Of course this is not a core doctrine of the faith and we can't be too dogmatic about it. If you disagree with this theory, that is perfectly okay.

But personally I believe that it is true. I believe that the death and resurrection of Jesus happened approximately 4,000 years from the date of creation, and I believe that there will be approximately 2,000 years from the death and resurrection of Jesus to His return.

The climactic events of the first coming of Jesus were prophetic fulfillments of the spring feasts, and as I discussed in *The Rapture Verdict*, I believe that the climactic events of the second coming of Jesus will be prophetic fulfillments of the fall feasts.

6000 years from creation, we are going to watch God do exactly what He said that He would do, and the most important end times events will take place during His appointed times.

Like I said, if you disagree with any of this that is not a problem at all. But I hope that you will keep an open mind as we proceed.

Psalm 90:4 is the first place in the Scriptures where a thousand years is specifically compared to one day...

For a thousand years in thy sight are but as yesterday when it is past, and as a watch in the night.

That verse could potentially be viewed a number of different ways, but the Apostle Peter was much more explicit. In 2 Peter, he wrote that "one day is as a thousand years, and a thousand years as one day", and he actually made that statement in the context of discussing the return of Jesus.

The following is what 2 Peter 3:8-10 says in the Modern English Version...

8 But, beloved, do not be ignorant of this one thing, that with the Lord one day is as a thousand years, and a thousand years as one day. 9 The Lord is not slow concerning His promise, as some count slowness. But He is patient with us, because He does not want any to perish, but all to come to repentance.

10 But the day of the Lord will come like a thief in the night, in which the heavens will pass away with a loud noise, and the elements will be destroyed with intense heat. The earth also and the works that are in it will be burned up.

You can believe that Peter was just being "symbolic" or "metaphorical" here, but I don't buy that.

He specifically warned us to "not be ignorant of this one thing" before telling us that a day is as a thousand years. If he was making a metaphorical statement that really didn't mean anything, why did he preface it in such a way?

In Hosea 6:1-2, there is a very interesting prophecy about "two days"...

Come, and let us return unto the Lord: for he hath torn, and he will heal us; he hath smitten, and he will bind us up.

2 After two days will he revive us: in the third day he will raise us up, and we shall live in his sight.

If the Millennial Day theory is correct, the Lord will indeed revive us at the rapture "after two days", and during the "third day" we will live in His presence.

If this prophecy does not refer to that, what else could it possibly mean?

In the next chapter I am going to share quotes from numerous early church leaders that believed in this theory, but it was also widely accepted long before the time of Christ.

For example, a belief in the Millennial Day theory is reflected in the Book of Jubilees. The following is what Jubilees 4:29-30 tells us...

"And at the close of the nineteenth jubilee, in the seventh week in the sixth year thereof, Adam died, and all his sons buried him in the land of his creation, and he was the first to be buried in the earth. And he lacked seventy years of one thousand years; for one thousand years are as one day in the testimony of the heavens and therefore was it written concerning the tree of knowledge: 'On the day that ye eat thereof ye shall die.' For this reason he did not complete the years of this day; for he died during it."

Of course Jubilees is not part of the Bible, but it is a book that was held in high regard by followers of the God of Israel before and after the time of Christ.

Before I end this chapter, I also want to point out that the return of the Lord Jesus is often connected to the start of "the Day of the Lord" in a number of places in the Scriptures.

In *The Rapture Verdict*, I explained that Joel chapter 2 is a description of Jesus returning with His army to defeat the forces of the Antichrist. In Joel 2:11, this event is connected with "the day of the Lord"...

And the Lord shall utter his voice before his army: for his camp is very great: for he is strong that executeth his word: for the day of the

Lord is great and very terrible; and who can abide it?

In Zechariah 14, the coming of the Day of the Lord is specifically linked with the moment when the feet of Jesus will touch down upon the Mount of Olives...

Behold, the day of the Lord cometh, and thy spoil shall be divided in the midst of thee.

2 For I will gather all nations against Jerusalem to battle; and the city shall be taken, and the houses rifled, and the women ravished; and half of the city shall go forth into captivity, and the residue of the people shall not be cut off from the city.

3 Then shall the Lord go forth, and fight against those nations, as when he fought in the day of battle.

4 And his feet shall stand in that day upon the mount of Olives, which is before Jerusalem on the east, and the mount of Olives shall cleave in the midst thereof toward the east and toward the west, and there shall be a very great valley; and half of the mountain shall remove toward the north, and half of it toward the south.

Once again, some scholars attempt to dismiss all of this by claiming that "the Day of the Lord" is a phrase which is simply "symbolic" or "metaphorical" and doesn't really mean anything.

But that doesn't make any sense to me.

Following his discussion about the resurrection of believers at the end of 1 Thessalonians chapter 4, the Apostle Paul warns that "the Day of the Lord" will come "as a thief in the night" at the beginning of 1 Thessalonians chapter 5...

But of the times and the seasons, brethren, ye have no need that I write unto you.

2 For yourselves know perfectly that the day of the Lord so cometh as a thief in the night.

3 For when they shall say, Peace and safety; then sudden destruction cometh upon them, as travail upon a woman with child; and they shall not escape.

4 But ye, brethren, are not in darkness, that that day should overtake you as a thief.

To me, it appears that the Apostle Paul is using "the Day of the Lord" as a technical term here, and he appears to assume that his readers will already know what he is talking about.

Unfortunately, these days most seminaries don't teach that "the Day of the Lord" could potentially mean a literal period of 1,000 years.

But once you connect "the Day of the Lord" with the Millennial reign, so many pieces of the puzzle start to fall into place.

In the portion of 2 Peter 3 that I quoted earlier in this chapter, the Apostle Peter also warned that "the Day of the Lord will come as a thief in the night". It is not just a coincidence that Paul and Peter used the exact same phrase.

And Peter used the phrase "the Day of the Lord" right after he told us that "one day is as a thousand years, and a thousand years as one day".

Liberal theologians would have us believe that there is absolutely no connection between "the Day of the Lord" and "one day is as a thousand years, and a thousand years as one day" even though the Apostle Peter uses the phrases just two verses apart.

Like I said earlier, I am entirely convinced that the Day of the Lord is 1,000 years long.

If we knew the exact year when Adam was created, we would be able to fast forward 6,000 years and determine exactly when the Day of the Lord should begin, but at this point we just don't know precisely when the events at the beginning of the Book of Genesis took place.

However, if the death and resurrection of Jesus took place approximately 4,000 years after creation (and that is a big assumption), that could help us to narrow things down quite a bit.

Today, there is a tremendous amount of debate about the precise year when Jesus died. We know that it happened on Passover, but scholars disagree about which Passover it was.

Throughout much of Christian history, it was assumed that Jesus died in 33 AD, and that is what I was taught growing up.

But over the past several decades a number of alternate theories have been put forward. Some claim that Jesus really died in 30 AD, others have suggested that 31 AD is the correct date, and yet others insist that 28 AD is the year when it happened.

Those appear to be the most common dates that are tossed around these days, but I have also seen additional theories that propose yet other years for the death of Christ.

What we can say with certainty is that the 2,000 year anniversary of the death of the Lord Jesus Christ is rapidly approaching. If that year will actually mark the 6,000 year anniversary of creation I believe that could be incredibly significant.

As I stated earlier, if the Millennial Day theory is accurate, that means that the 7 year apocalypse and the Millennial reign of

Christ are nearly upon us.

As time goes by, things should become a lot clearer, and I plan to update my findings in future books.

In the next chapter, I am going to share a long list of quotes that show that many leaders of the early church also believed in the Millennial Day theory...

THE EARLY CHURCH AND THE SABBATH MILLENNIUM

In the last chapter, I briefly outlined the Millennial Day theory, and I mentioned the fact that it has been widely believed among prominent Christian leaders throughout history. In this chapter, we are going to take a look at this in detail. Just because I am quoting them, I don't want you to get the impression that I endorse everything that these early church leaders believed. In some cases, they veered significantly away from the faith that was handed down by the original apostles. I am simply quoting them so that you can understand that the Millennial Day theory has been around for a very long time and was widely believed during the days of the early church.

Let's start with Irenaeus. If you are not familiar with him, Irenaeus was a disciple of Polycarp who in turn had been a disciple of the Apostle John. His most famous treatise, *Against Heresies*, was written in 180 AD and it remains one of the most famous works of the early church to this day.

In *Against Heresies*, Irenaeus clearly linked the days of creation to God's seven thousand year plan for humanity...

For in as many days as this world was made, in so many thousand years shall it be concluded. And for this reason the Scripture says: Thus the heaven and the earth were finished, and all their adornment. And God brought to a conclusion upon the sixth day the works that He had made; and God rested upon the seventh day from all His works. This is an account of the things formerly created, as also it is a prophecy of what is to come. For the day of the Lord is as a thousand years; and in six days created things were completed: it is evident, therefore, that they will come to an end at the sixth thousand year.

For Irenaeus, the number six represented man's rebellion against God, and so he felt that it was quite appropriate that humanity's apostasy would last for exactly six thousand years...

And there is therefore in this beast, when he comes, a recapitulation made of all sorts of iniquity and of every deceit, in order that all apostate power, flowing into and being shut up in him, may be sent into the furnace of fire. Fittingly, therefore, shall his name possess the number six hundred and sixty-six, since he sums up in his own person all the commixture of wickedness which took place previous to the deluge, due to the apostasy of the angels. For Noah was six hundred years old when the deluge came upon the earth, sweeping away the rebellious world, for the sake of that most infamous generation which lived in the times of Noah. And [Antichrist] also sums up every error of devised idols since the flood, together with the slaying of the prophets and the cutting off of the just. For that image which was set up by Nebuchadnezzar had indeed a height of sixty cubits, while the breadth was six cubits; on account of which Ananias, Azarias, and Misael, when they did not worship it, were cast into a furnace of fire, pointing out prophetically, by what happened to them, the wrath against the righteous which shall arise towards the [time of the] end. For that image, taken as a whole, was a prefiguring of this man's coming, decreeing that he should undoubtedly himself alone be worshipped by all men. Thus, then, the six hundred years of Noah, in whose time the deluge occurred because of the apostasy, and the number of the cubits of the image for which these just men were sent into the fiery furnace, do indicate the number of the name of that man in whom is concentrated the whole apostasy of six thousand years...

I was amazed when I first came across these quotes. To Irenaeus, it was exceedingly clear that a thousand years represented a "day" on God's timeline, and he went all the way back to Adam for evidence to help make that point...

Thus, then, in the day that they ate, in the same did they die, and became death's debtors, since it was one day of the creation. For it is said, There was made in the evening, and there was made in the morning, one day. Now in this same day that they ate, in that also did they die. But according to the cycle and progress of the days, after which one is termed first, another second, and another third, if anybody seeks diligently to learn upon what day out of the seven it was that Adam died, he will find it by examining the dispensation of the Lord. For by summing up in Himself the whole human race from the beginning to the end, He has also summed up its death. From this it is clear that the Lord suffered death, in obedience to His Father, upon that day on which Adam died while he disobeyed God. Now he died on the same day in which he ate. For God said, In that day on which you shall eat of it, you shall die by death. The Lord, therefore, recapitulating in Himself this day, underwent His sufferings upon the day preceding the Sabbath, that is, the sixth day of the creation, on which day man was created; thus granting him a second creation by means of His passion, which is that [creation] out of death. And there are some, again, who relegate the death of Adam to the thousandth year; for since a day of the Lord is as a thousand years, he did not overstep the thousand years, but died within them, thus bearing out the sentence of his sin. Whether, therefore, with respect to disobedience, which is death; whether [we consider] that, on account of that, they were delivered over to death, and made debtors to it; whether with respect to [the fact that on] one and the same day on which they ate they also died (for it is one day of the creation); whether [we regard this point], that, with respect to this cycle of days, they died on the day in which they did also eat, that is, the day of the preparation, which is termed the pure supper, that is, the sixth day of the feast, which the Lord also exhibited when He suffered on that day; or whether [we reflect] that he (Adam) did not overstep the thousand years, but died within their limit — it follows that, in regard to all these significations, God is indeed true. For they died who tasted of the tree; and the serpent is proved a liar and a murderer, as the Lord said of him: For he is a murderer from the beginning, and the truth is not in him.

Of course Irenaeus was definitely not the only prominent voice in the early church to address this issue.

The following is a sampling of quotes from other early church leaders that also believed in the Millennial Day theory...

The Epistle Of Barnabas (written some time between 70 and 132 AD)

Further, also, it is written concerning the Sabbath in the Decalogue which [the Lord] spoke, face to face, to Moses on Mount Sinai, "And sanctify ye the Sabbath of the Lord with clean hands and a pure heart." And He says in another place, "If my sons keep the Sabbath, then will I cause my mercy to rest upon them." The Sabbath is mentioned at the beginning of the creation [thus]: "And God made in six days the works of His hands, and made an end on the seventh day, and rested on it, and sanctified it." Attend, my children, to the meaning of this expression, "He finished in six days." This implieth that the Lord will finish all things in six thousand years, for a day is with Him a thousand years. And He Himself testifieth, saying, "Behold, to-day will be as a thousand years." Therefore, my children, in six days, that is, in six thousand years, all things will be finished. "And He rested on the seventh day." This meaneth: when His Son, coming [again], shall destroy the time of the wicked man, and judge the ungodly, and change the-sun, and the moon, and the stars, then shall He truly rest on the seventh day.

Justin Martyr (100 AD - 165 AD)

For Isaiah spake thus concerning this space of a thousand years: 'For there shall be the new heaven and the new earth, and the former shall not be remembered, or come into their heart; but they shall find joy and gladness in it, which things I create. For, behold, I make Jerusalem a rejoicing, and My people a joy; and I shall rejoice over Jerusalem, and be glad over My people. And the voice of weeping shall be no more heard in her, or the voice of crying. And there shall be no more there a person of immature years, or an old man who shall not fulfil his days. For the young man shall be an hundred years old; but the sinner who dies an hundred years old, he shall be accursed. And they shall build houses, and shall themselves inhabit them; and they shall plant vines, and shall themselves eat the produce of them, and drink the wine. They shall not build, and others inhabit; they shall not plant, and others eat. For according to the days of the tree of life shall be the days of my people; the works of their toil shall abound. Mine elect shall not toil fruitlessly, or beget children to be cursed; for they shall be a seed righteous and blessed by the Lord, and their offspring with them. And it shall come to pass, that before they call I will hear; while they are still speaking, I shall say, What is it? Then shall the wolves and the lambs feed together, and the lion shall eat straw like the ox; but the serpent [shall eat] earth as bread. They shall not hurt or maltreat each other on the holy mountain, saith the Lord.' Now we have understood that the expression used among these words, 'According to the days of the tree [of life] shall be the days of my people; the works of their toil shall abound,' obscurely predicts a thousand years. For as Adam was told that in the day he ate of the tree he would die, we know that he did not complete a thousand years. We have perceived, moreover, that the expression, 'The day of the Lord is as a thousand years,' is connected with this subject. And further, there was a certain man with us, whose name was John, one of the apostles of Christ, who prophesied, by a revelation that was made to him, that those who believed in our Christ would dwell a thousand years in Jerusalem; and that thereafter the general, and, in short, the eternal resurrection and judgment of all men would likewise take place. Just as our Lord also said, 'They shall neither marry nor be given in marriage, but shall be equal to the angels, the children of the God of the resurrection.'

Hippolytus (170 AD - 235 AD)

For the Sabbath is the type and emblem of the future kingdom of the saints, when they "shall reign with Christ," when He comes from heaven, as John says in his Apocalypse: for "a day with the Lord is as a thousand years." Since, then, in six days God made all things, it follows that 6,000 years must be fulfilled.

Cyprian (200 AD - 258 AD)

The first seven days in the divine arrangement contain seven thousand years.

Victorinus (250 - 303 AD)

Wherefore to those seven days the Lord attributed to each a thousand years; for thus went the warning: "In Thine eyes, O Lord, a thousand years are as one day." Therefore in the eyes of the Lord each thousand of years is ordained, for I find that the Lord's eyes are seven. Wherefore, as I have narrated, that true Sabbath will be in the seventh millenary of years, when Christ with His elect shall reign.

Lactantius (240 AD - 320 AD)

Therefore, since all the works of God were completed in six days, the world must continue in its present state through six ages, that is, six thousand years. For the great day of God is limited by a circle of a thousand years, as the prophet shows, who says "In Thy sight, O Lord, a thousand years are as one day." And as God laboured during those six days in creating such great works, so His religion and truth must labour during these six thousand years, while wickedness prevails and bears rule. And again, since God, having finished His works, rested the seventh day and blessed it, at the end of the six thousandth year all wickedness must be abolished from the earth, and righteousness reign for a thousand years; and there must be tranquillity and rest from the labours which the world now has long endured. But how that will come to pass I will explain in its order. We have often said that lesser things and things of small importance are figures and previous shadowings forth of great things; as this day of ours, which is bounded by the rising and the setting of the sun, is a representation of that great day to which the circuit of a thousand years affixes its limits.

Methodius (written in approximately 300 AD)

For since in six days God made the heaven and the earth, and finished the whole world, and rested on the seventh day from all His works which He had made, and blessed the seventh day and sanctified it, so by a figure in the seventh month, when the fruits of the earth have been gathered in, we are commanded to keep the feast to the Lord, which signifies that, when this world shall be terminated at the seventh thousand years, when God shall have completed the world, He shall rejoice in us.

Commodianus (300 - 360 AD)

This has pleased Christ, that the dead should rise again, yea, with their bodies; and those, too, whom in this world the fire has burned, when six thousand years are completed, and the world has come to an end.

Needless to say, just because a lot of leaders in the early church believed something does not mean that it is true.

But I wanted to show all of you that this is something that Christian leaders have believed since the very beginning.

This isn't a new doctrine that someone just dreamed up fairly recently. All along, Christians have been looking forward to the Day of the Lord at the conclusion of six thousand years, and now we have finally reached a point when we are almost there.

SIGNS OF THE TIMES

So much has transpired since I released my last book. In this chapter, I want to give you an update on many of the prophetic events that were addressed in *Lost Prophecies Of The Future Of America*, because it is so important for people to realize that these things are coming quickly. We really are living in the end times, and I believe that global events will soon accelerate greatly.

Let's talk about war first. Jesus said that the end times would be marked by "wars and rumors of wars", and recent months have certainly been a time of "rumors of wars".

When Russia rushed more than 100,000 troops toward the conflict zone with Ukraine, there were fears that an invasion was imminent. And even though things appear to have cooled down for the moment, a war between Russia and Ukraine could still literally erupt at any time.

Of course if Russia and Ukraine do go to war, the United States is not going to sit on the sidelines.

In my last book, I featured a large number of prophetic voices that have warned that someday the United States and Russia will go to war. But we don't know what specifically will spark that conflict.

Could it be possible that it will be Ukraine? I don't know, but I am definitely watching developments over there very, very closely.

Meanwhile, U.S. relations with China continue to rapidly deteri-orate. The protests in Hong Kong and the status of the South China Sea were major sources of tension during the Trump ad-ministration, but now the possibility that Taiwan may formally declare independence has taken center stage. If Taiwan tries to formally declare independence, the Chinese have warned that they will invade, and the United States has made it quite clear that such an invasion will not be tolerated.

For those that have read my last book, you already know that many prophetic voices have been shown that someday the U.S. and China will go to war.

In fact, Dumitru Duduman was specifically told that "when America goes to war with China, the Russians will strike with-out warning."

So we are watching for a U.S. war with China, and such a conflict is now closer than it has been at any point since the end of the Korean War.

If President Trump had remained in office, I do not think that we would be at this point. Even though Trump could be tough with other nations, he was also quite eager to avoid any new military conflicts.

The Biden administration, on the other hand, has taken a com-pletely different approach. Biden administration officials seem determined to exert U.S. influence all over the globe very force-fully, but other countries are not intimidated by the U.S. in the same way that they once were.

Joe Biden has always been a hothead, but now he is a hothead that is in an advanced state of cognitive decline.

And he has literally surrounded himself with an all-star team of warmongers. Most Americans don't realize this, but Biden's foreign policy team makes George W. Bush's foreign policy team look like a bunch of peace-loving hippies. Biden administration officials are being extremely aggressive with both Russia and China, and if they push too far they may cross a point of no return.

Foreign policy requires a great deal of finesse. It is absolutely critical to be tough, but being too tough can have absolutely catastrophic consequences.

Unfortunately, we know where all of this is heading. Whether it is sooner or later, global war is coming, and it is not going to end well for us.

Meanwhile, a major war could erupt in the Middle East at any moment. I spent an entire chapter talking about this in my last book, and by the time you read this book it may have already started.

In particular, the coming war between Israel and Iran appears to be closer than ever.

As I write this book, the Iranians continue to feverishly develop their nuclear program, and the Israelis have pledged that they will never, ever allow the Iranians to get to the point where they can produce their own nuclear weapons.

The recent cyberattack that greatly disrupted operations at the Natanz nuclear facility was a significant setback for the Iranians, but it only slowed them down.

It certainly didn't stop them.

Israeli airstrikes on pro-Iranian forces in Syria continue to become more frequent, and everyone knows that the "mystery explosions" that have been happening inside Iran from time to time are the work of Israel.

The Iranians have responded by attacking multiple Israeli cargo ships, although the Iranians are officially denying responsibility for those attacks.

This "shadow war" between Israel and Iran will transition into a full-blown shooting war eventually. At some point someone will decide to push things too far, and then missiles will start flying back and forth between the two nations.

It will be a truly, truly horrible war, and it will shock the entire globe.

In my last book I also went into quite a bit of detail about the great seismic events that are coming. Unfortunately, since I published that book the crust of our planet has just continued to become more unstable. So far this year we have seen a lot more large earthquakes than we did during the same period of time last year, and once dormant volcanoes continue to roar to life all over the planet.

But what we have experienced so far is nothing compared to the shaking that is still to come.

Something dramatic appears to be happening to the globe. Massive sinkholes have suddenly been appearing in a whole bunch of different countries, buildings and bridges are suddenly collapsing, weather patterns are going absolutely nuts, and water levels are rising to unexpected levels in many areas. As I discover more about the strange changes that are happening to our planet, I plan to discuss this in more detail in future books.

Of course the Bible told us in advance that things would get really crazy during this time. Jesus specifically warned us that there would be earthquakes in "diverse places" in the last days, and every man, woman and child on the entire planet will be greatly affected as our world is rattled like never before.

As great seismic events rock the planet, and as global weather patterns continue to shift dramatically, global food production is going to be thrown into a state of chaos. The head of the UN World Food Program has warned that we are moving into a time when there will be "famines of biblical proportions", and initially it will be the poorest parts of the planet that suffer the most.

But as I detailed in my last book, eventually there will be great famines virtually everywhere, including the United States of America.

Most Americans can't even imagine what a famine would look like. Throughout our entire lives, we have always been able to go to the stores and buy as much food as we want. To the vast majority of us, a famine inside the U.S. is absolutely unthinkable.

But it is coming. John Paul Jackson was shown that Dust Bowl conditions would return, and that is actually happening right now. Scientists tell us that the western half of the country is in a multi-year "megadrought", and 2021 has been the worst year of that megadrought so far.

Needless to say, this "megadrought" is having an enormous impact on farmers, and U.S. agricultural production will be significantly lower than anticipated this year.

And just like the original Dust Bowl, this "megadrought" is causing dust storms of colossal size. In fact, some of them have been so large that you can actually see them from space.

But you don't hear about this much from the corporate media, do you?

No, they are way too busy covering the latest political scandals.

Right now, water levels in Lake Powell and Lake Mead are dropping precipitously. It is being projected that both will soon hit all-time record lows, and that could mean very serious water restrictions for much of the southwestern United States.

Is it just a coincidence that all of these things are occurring simultaneously?

And is it just a coincidence that so many prophetic voices were shown all of these things well in advance?

An increase in persecution is another topic that I tackled in my last book, and that is a trend that has definitely accelerated in recent months.

The U.S. Commission on International Religious Freedom just released a report that is sounding the alarm about what is going on around the globe, and one expert that worked on the report recently stated that "Christians are being persecuted around the world at a pace not seen since the first century".

That definitely got my attention.

In China, the persecution of believers is reaching very frightening levels. Over the past couple of years countless underground churches have been raided and shut down, the online sale of Bibles has been banned and physical Bibles have been regularly burned in the streets, and Christians that won't cooperate with the government are taken to secretive "transformation" facilities where they are ordered to renounce their faith.

Those that refuse to renounce their faith are endlessly beaten and tortured. Survivors that have come forward tell us that this can happen for months on end.

Would you be willing to suffer beatings and torture for months for the sake of Christ?

You need to make that decision now, because the global persecution of Christians will be absolutely horrific when the Antichrist finally comes on the scene.

Chapter ten in *Lost Prophecies of the Future of America* is all about what the prophetic voices have been shown regarding the coming persecution of believers. But most of those that fill the pews of our churches today are not mentally preparing themselves to face such persecution, because they have been promised that they will be pulled out of here before we ever get to that point.

When millions upon millions of believers realize that they are still here to face such persecution, the despair is going to be off the charts.

But that is not how we should look at it.

In the Book of Acts, believers rejoiced that they were counted worthy to suffer for the cause of Christ.

If we are born again, our destiny is to be with the Lord forever, and that is worth sacrificing everything for.

Jesus laid down His life for us.

Are we willing to lay down our lives for Him?

No matter how long you can make it last, this life is just temporary, and the things of this world that we are all so busy chasing are just temporary.

But the things that we do for God can matter for eternity.

Don't live for what is temporary. Live for what is eternal, because what is eternal is what really matters.

Before I end this chapter, there is one more thing that I would like to discuss.

In Matthew 24, Jesus told us that "pestilences" would be one of the signs that His return was approaching. We are in the midst of the COVID pandemic right now, and authorities are telling us that we should be deeply alarmed by the "Delta variant" that emerged in India and that is now spreading all over the globe. Over time, we shall see how deadly "Delta" and other new variants prove to be, but what I am far more concerned about is the next pandemic.

As I warned in my last book, prophetic voices have seen that another pandemic is coming, and it will be much worse than the COVID pandemic.

This is one thing that we are still waiting for, and hopefully it will not have started by the time you read this book.

As I have been reflecting on the order of events in the first half of the Tribulation, I have been wondering whether this next pandemic might be unleashed during the fourth seal. This is what Revelation 6:7-8 says in the New International Version...

7 When the Lamb opened the fourth seal, I heard the voice of the fourth living creature say, "Come!" 8 I looked, and there before me was a pale horse! Its rider was named Death, and Hades was following close behind him. They were given power over a fourth of the earth to kill by sword, famine and plague, and by the wild beasts of the earth.

Could it be possible that the "plague" referred to in these verses is the next great pandemic?

I don't know, but if it is, then we should expect certain other things to happen first.

The second seal brings the outbreak of war, and the third seal brings economic collapse. During a time of war and great economic chaos, it would be really easy for disease to spread like wildfire, and the Scriptures tell us that an unprecedented number of people will die.

Of course I can't prove any direct connection between the fourth seal and the next pandemic right now. At this point, I am just speculating.

As I have always said, the closer that we get to prophetic events the clearer the prophetic Scriptures will become for all of us.

But without a doubt, God wants us to study the Scriptures that apply to our times, and Jesus specifically ordered us to watch for signs of His return.

Unfortunately, most believers are dead asleep right now, and that is extremely unfortunate.

A GIANT "X" ACROSS AMERICA

If you were to mark a giant "X" across something, what would that mean?

Obviously, it is normally not a very good sign.

If I have a list of things that I am considering, I may use an "X" to eliminate options that are no longer viable.

Or if I have a list of things that I am supposed to do, I will often mark an "X" across an item to indicate that it is finished or completed.

An "X" can "mark the spot" on a treasure hunt, but it can also be a warning sign of danger.

According to dictionary.com, using a big "X" on the Internet "generally communicates warnings, errors, and undesirability" and in the sports world it is often used "to denote a 'strike' in baseball, a missed scoring attempt generally, or a lost match."

As you can see from all of these examples, an "X" tends to signify some sort of a final outcome.

So why am I sharing all of this?

Well, what would you say if I told you that an enormous "X" that is in the process of being marked across the United States will be completed in the year 2024?

I know that may sound very strange, but stick with me and you will soon understand what I am talking about.

On August 21st, 2017 the "Great American Eclipse" made headlines all over the world. It was the very first solar eclipse since 1918 that was able to be seen all the way from the west coast to the east coast. In the U.S., the path of the eclipse started in Oregon, it continued all the way across the continental United States, and it exited the country in South Carolina.

But what makes that eclipse unlike any other is the fact that it will combine with another historic eclipse in 2024 to form a giant "X" across America.

On April 8th, 2024 another "Great American Eclipse" will make headlines all over the planet. The path of that eclipse will cross over the states of Texas, Oklahoma, Arkansas, Missouri, Illinois, Kentucky, Tennessee, Michigan, Indiana, Ohio, Pennsylvania, New York, Vermont, New Hampshire and Maine. If you plot the paths of the 2017 eclipse and the 2024 eclipse on the same map, you will clearly see that they combine to form a massive "X" right over the heartland of the continental United States.

Could it be possible that this is some sort of a sign?

In the Scriptures, Jesus clearly tells us that "there shall be signs in the sun, and in the moon, and in the stars" in the last days. In fact, this is what Luke 21:25-26 tells us in the King James Version...

25 And there shall be signs in the sun, and in the moon, and in the stars; and upon the earth distress of nations, with perplexity; the sea and the waves roaring;

26 Men's hearts failing them for fear, and for looking after those things which are coming on the earth: for the powers of heaven shall be shaken.

So if Christ's return is drawing near, we would expect for there to be some pretty remarkable signs in the heavens.

And if you ask me, I think that a giant "X" being written across our nation is a pretty remarkable sign.

But there is even more to the story.

December 14th, 2020 was exactly halfway between the "Great American Eclipse" of 2017 and the "Great American Eclipse" of 2024.

Of course that was the date when the Electoral College voted to elect Joe Biden the president of the United States.

In our system of government, the American people do not directly elect the president. Instead, we go to the polls and vote for slates of "electors" in each state, and at a later date those electors cast their votes for president.

Whether you like the Electoral College or not, that is how our system of government works, and so nobody can become the "president-elect" until the Electoral College holds the presidential election.

Once the Electoral College voted, the mainstream media told us that it "sealed" Joe Biden's victory, and for those of us that believe that the election was not conducted honestly that was a very sad day in American history.

Because if we no longer have free and fair elections, there is no future for our system of government.

And of course with Joe Biden and Kamala Harris in the White House, our federal government will boldly promote and celebrate the very things that will ultimately bring the judgment of God upon this nation.

So is it just a coincidence that December 14th, 2020 happened to mark the exact midpoint between the two great eclipses which will combine to form a giant "X" over our nation?

I think that is a very good question. Unfortunately, very few people are talking about this.

A number of other very unusual things also took place on December 14th, 2020. The Geminid meteor shower peaked, Comet Erasmus was visible from our planet for a very short period of time, and the only solar eclipse of the entire year just happened to fall on that date.

It was almost as if somebody out there was trying really hard to get our attention.

Sadly, I didn't see any other prominent Christian websites publish articles about these amazing connections.

There is still one more aspect of all of this that I have not discussed yet.

The exact intersection formed by the Great American Eclipse of 2017 and the Great American Eclipse of 2024 covers portions of the states of Kentucky, Illinois and Missouri.

If you examine this area on a map, you will quickly discover that it is right in the middle of the New Madrid fault zone.

In my previous book entitled *"Lost Prophecies Of The Future Of*

America", I shared numerous examples of people that have had supernatural experiences in which God showed them the absolutely massive earthquake that will strike the region someday. It will literally divide the country in half physically from the Great Lakes to the Gulf of Mexico. In fact, the rift that will be created will be so vast that it will actually form an entirely new body of water. In order to get across it, you will need to fly, because all existing roads and bridges from east to west will have been destroyed by the giant quake.

Of course we could see smaller quakes in the region at any time. So if a magnitude 6, 7 or 8 earthquake happens along the New Madrid fault zone, please don't think that it is the "big event" and that all of the prophecies have now been fulfilled.

The absolutely massive quake that so many people have been shown will not happen until after the land of Israel is officially divided. As I shared in my last book, God has specifically warned that the physical division of our land will be a consequence for the U.S. government being involved in formally dividing the land of Israel.

This is why I always make such a big fuss whenever there is a new effort to divide the land of Israel. This is a red line that must never, ever be crossed, but most Christians simply do not understand how seriously God takes these things.

I wish that more preachers would take a very strong stand against dividing the land of Israel, because once it happens there will be no going back.

Most of those living in the New Madrid fault zone don't even realize how vulnerable the region is. It sits directly on top of a very deep geological scar that was formed when the continent of North America was shifting into place. According to Wikipedia, this colossal scar makes "the Earth's crust in the New Madrid area mechanically weaker than much of the rest of North America".

The San Andreas fault zone gets a lot more attention from the mainstream media, but the New Madrid fault zone is actually six times larger and has the potential to create far more powerful seismic events.

In fact, the largest earthquakes to ever happen in the continental United States have occurred along the New Madrid fault zone.

All the way back in 1811 and 1812, the New Madrid fault zone produced four enormous quakes that we still talk about today. Thousands of very deep fissures ripped open fields, the Mississippi River actually ran backwards in certain places, and people could feel the quakes as far away as Washington D.C. and Boston.

And scientists assure us that someday such an earthquake will happen again.

If you live in the states of Illinois, Indiana, Ohio, Missouri, Arkansas, Kentucky, Tennessee and Mississippi, you are potentially in danger.

But the event that will literally tear the United States in two will not happen until the U.S. is involved in formally dividing the land of Israel. So that is a key prophetic signpost that we are watching for.

And it is important for me to note that we don't know exactly how soon the New Madrid quake will happen after there is an agreement to divide the land of Israel.

It could be a day, a month, a year or even longer.

We just don't know.

But as certain as you are reading this, it will happen.

Once the land of Israel is formally divided, you will want to make a decision about which side of the New Madrid fault zone you want to be on, because you might not be able to get back across to the other side for the foreseeable future.

Of course we should all want to see these catastrophic events delayed for as long as possible, and so I would encourage you to pray that our politicians would be frustrated in their attempts to divide the land of Israel.

Unfortunately, it appears that another major push to divide the land may soon happen, and that is very bad news.

Could it be possible that the giant "X" formed by the two eclipses in 2017 and 2024 represents yet another warning from God that we should not mess with the Holy Land?

Once again, I want to be very clear that I am not setting any dates. We do not know what significance 2024 may have if any.

Perhaps we have been given this period of time to repent and if that does not happen we will suffer some very severe consequences some time after 2024.

I wish that I had all the answers for you, but without a doubt I believe that this giant "X" should be getting our attention.

All throughout human history, God has sent warnings before bringing judgment, and in our time He has been warning us in a whole host of different ways.

Sadly, most of the U.S. population has chosen to totally ignore the warnings, and now the hour is very, very late.

AMERICA IN DECLINE

At the very outset of this chapter, I just want to state for the record that I deeply love the United States of America.

Because I often write so harshly about the current condition of the United States, and because I write about such horrible things that are going to happen to this country, a lot of people assume that I must want America to fail.

Of course that is not true at all. When I was growing up, I developed a great love for this nation. My father served in the U.S. Navy, and I have always been deeply patriotic. I ran for Congress because I wanted to be part of an effort to turn this country around, and I have been calling for America to repent for many, many years.

I grew up in the 1970s. Life was so much simpler back then, and I mean that in a very good way. Even though society was changing, in those days it could generally be said that men were still men and women were still women. Americans valued faith, family and the flag, and even most people that didn't go to church typically tried to abide by the overall moral standards of the day. We regarded ourselves as "the good guys", and the godless communist radicals on the other side of the globe were "the bad guys".

Sadly, at this point we have become the godless communist radicals.

For decades, there has been an epic struggle for control of America's values. This epic struggle is often called "the culture war", and it is often framed in political terms, but the reality of the matter is that it runs much deeper than that.

Every moment of every day, a relentless battle is being waged for the minds of the American people. Just about everything that you watch on television, listen to on the radio and look at on the Internet is designed to shape how you view the world. Once you realize this, you will start to notice cultural messaging in just about every form of "programming" that you consume.

Today, the average American watches 238 minutes of television a day.

If you allow anyone to pump that much "programming" into your mind on a daily basis, it is going to dramatically affect how you view the world.

At this point, more than 90 percent of the "news" that Americans watch on television is controlled by just five giant corporations, and those five giant corporations are controlled by the elite of the world.

Needless to say, this gives the elite an enormous amount of influence over the direction our country is going.

Our education system has also been totally taken over by the left, and it has become one of their most powerful tools in the culture war. Each new generation has become more "progressive", and I am about to share some numbers with you that show this very clearly. Relentless indoctrination takes place from kindergarten all the way through the highest levels of university education, and so the longer that our children stay in the mainstream education system the more likely it is that they will adopt leftist views.

Once they get out into the "real world", our kids quickly realize that our economy is now completely and totally dominated by giant corporations. Needless to say, many of those giant corporations have now become eager participants in the culture war as well. If you do not align with the agendas that they are pushing, you will not be allowed to move up the ranks even if you do manage to land a job with one of them.

Of course most of the big corporations are owned by the same global elitists that also own the media conglomerates that are endlessly pumping propaganda into the heads of everyone around us.

So even though we call it a "culture war", one side has vastly more power and vastly more money than the other side does.

Unfortunately, all of that power and all of that money has caused a dramatic shift in how Americans view the world over the years.

Let's start by taking a look at support for gay marriage. If you go all the way back to 1988, a University of Chicago poll found that only 11 percent of Americans supported same-sex marriage, with 68 percent opposing it.

To say that there was a general consensus in society at that time would be a major understatement.

But then the numbers began to shift, and in 2009 an ABC News/ Washington Post poll found that supporters of gay marriage outnumbered opponents for the very first time. It was just 49 percent to 46 percent, but everyone could see that the tide was definitely turning.

Today, Americans are overwhelmingly in favor of gay marriage. According to the 11th annual American Values Survey, 70 percent of all Americans now support gay marriage, and only 28 percent of Americans are opposed.

Those numbers are absolutely staggering.

To go from 11 percent in the polls to 70 percent in just 33 years is a monumental shift.

At this point, it is safe to say that one side is winning the "culture war" on that particular issue and one side is losing.

The number of Americans that identify as LGBT has been steadily rising as well. Today it is at an all-time record high, but the real story is what the numbers look like when we break it down by generation.

According to Gallup, this is the share of each generation that currently identifies as LGBT...

Generation Z (born 1997-2002): 15.9 percent

Millennials (born 1981-1996): 9.1 percent

Generation X (born 1965-1980): 3.8 percent

Baby boomers (born 1946-1964): 2.0 percent

Traditionalists (born before 1946): 1.3 percent

Just look at those numbers.

Compared to the oldest Americans, those that are members of Generation Z are more than 10 times as likely as to identify as LGBT.

Wow.

Something else that really shocked me about the Gallup survey was that it discovered that a whopping 54.6 percent of all LGBT adults say that they identify as bisexual.

That means that a majority of LGBT adults in the United States freely admit that they are attracted to both men and women.

Abortion is another one of the most hotly debated issues in the "culture war".

For years, pro-life activists have been working very hard to get Americans to understand that killing babies in the womb is morally wrong, but once again the other side has far more power and far more money and it shows.

According to a survey that was released by NBC News last year, 66 percent of U.S. adults want to keep Roe v. Wade in place, and only 29 percent of Americans want it to be overturned.

That means that Americans support Roe v. Wade by a more than two to one margin.

You could say that this is just one poll result, but many other polls have come up with similar numbers.

Sadly, with each passing year older Americans with more socially conservative beliefs are dying off, and they are being replaced by younger Americans that tend to be much more liberal on social issues.

Without a doubt, this has huge implications for the future of our society. Compared to when I was growing up, Americans are far more likely to believe that sex outside of marriage is morally acceptable, they are far more likely to get a sexually-transmitted disease, they are far more likely to put off marriage, they are far more likely to not get married at all, and they are far more likely to reject the idea that children need two parents.

In fact, one recent survey discovered that an all-time record low 68.9 percent of all U.S. children are being raised in a home that includes two parents.

That means that nearly a third of all American children are missing at least one parent, and if one parent is missing from the home it is usually the father.

And a whole host of studies have shown that children that are raised in a home without a father are much more likely to commit serious crimes and are much more likely to fall into poverty.

In fact, 90 percent of all prison inmates in America today grew up in a home without a father.

What I have shared in this chapter is just the tip of the iceberg. Over the years, I have shared hundreds and hundreds of statistics that clearly show that America is in a deep state of moral and social decline.

The only hope that our country has of reversing course is to turn to Jesus, but that isn't happening.

In fact, most young Americans are running away from God as fast as they possibly can.

When I was growing up, I would read the parts in the Bible where it would talk about how ancient Israel fell away from God at various times, and it always puzzled me how something like that could happen so rapidly.

Well, now I know, because I have seen it happen right in front of my eyes.

America has willingly chosen to reject God, and the consequences for this decision are going to deeply affect all of us.

THE VOLCANO DREAM

On the morning of May 8th, 2021 I had an extremely vivid dream which had a very deep impact on me emotionally. Everything that I experienced in the dream felt like it was really happening. In fact, in the dream when I thought that I was about to die, in that moment I truly believed with every fiber of my being that I was about to die. The events were so real, the emotions were so real, and it is an experience that I will never forget.

I don't know where I was located in the dream, but it wasn't where I currently live. I think that the dream was set at night or in the early morning, but for reasons that I will explain I can't say for sure. My wife Meranda was with me during the events of the dream, and my concern for her safety only heightened the emotional impact of this dream.

In the dream I was suddenly alerted to the fact that a major volcanic eruption had just happened. When I looked outside, the skies were obscured by volcanic ash, and that is why I could not tell for sure at what time of day the dream took place. As I looked off in the distance, I noticed that an enormous tsunami of volcanic ash was coming right at us. It was coming our direction very rapidly, and there was nothing else that could be done except to brace for impact. I started yelling at Meranda and everyone else in the vicinity to take cover. The structure that we were staying in had two levels, and we went to the lower level and I was yelling for everyone to "get down". I glanced up at the massive tsunami of volcanic ash that was coming at us, and I truly believed that we would not survive.

The volcanic ash hit our structure and the surrounding structures with tremendous violence. Along with the tsunami of volcanic ash came very high winds. Even though I was certain that we would perish, somehow we survived.

Not too long after that, giant balls of fire began falling from the sky all around us. I understood that they had been ejected from the volcano, and when they hit they started multitudes of little fires which soon became bigger fires.

Pretty soon there were massive fires all around us. I knew that we had to get out of there, but I didn't know which direction to go. Even though we had made it through the tsunami of volcanic ash, I was certain that we would die in the fires.

But that didn't happen. Suddenly rain started to fall, and miraculously it put out all of the fires.

Unfortunately, the seismic activity didn't stop. I knew that we were still in great danger from the volcano, and I was extremely concerned about what was coming next.

I didn't have to wait too long to find out. There were numerous structures in the area where we were staying, and in an open space that was not occupied by any building all of a sudden a giant rock formation began to emerge out of the ground very rapidly.

It just kept growing and it shook everything around us. In this instance, I did not think that we were going to die, but the violence with which this giant rock formation was climbing into the sky took my breath away.

I woke up shortly after, and as I was preparing for the day it was impressed upon me that this was a dream that I needed to share.

This dream caused me to reflect on a couple of major prophetic events which are coming in our future. One of them is the future eruption of Mt. Rainier.

Those that follow my articles on a regular basis already know that I have been warning about Mt. Rainier for quite a few years. It is regarded as "the most dangerous mountain in America" because it is located so close to major population centers.

Many Americans remember the eruption of Mount St. Helens in 1980, but Mt. Rainier is about twice the size of Mount St. Helens, and millions of people live within viewing distance.

When it finally blows, large numbers of people will find themselves in imminent danger.

Scientists tell us that Mt. Rainier is capable of producing giant tsunamis of super-heated mud known as lahars. These lahars can be hundreds of feet high and they can travel at speeds of up to 50 miles per hour.

Thankfully, Mt. Rainier hasn't produced any lahars since the U.S. became a nation, but scientists assure us that it is just a matter of time before it happens again.

Unfortunately, this long period of inactivity has lulled us into a false sense of security, and vast numbers of people now live in communities that have been constructed on top of the danger zone.

I don't think that what I saw in my dream was a lahar. If a lahar were to hit your home, everyone and everything inside would be instantly cooked and permanently buried in blazing hot mud.

According to the USGS, approximately 150,000 people currently live on top of old lahar deposits from Mt. Rainier.

Needless to say, that was not very smart planning.

Experts tell us that Mt. Rainier is capable of producing lahars that would utterly destroy Enumclaw, Buckley, Orting, Kent, Auburn, Puyallup, Sumner and Renton. Tacoma would be in great danger as well, and there is a possibility that a lahar from Mt. Rainier could even devastate portions of downtown Seattle.

The death and destruction such an event would cause would be unlike anything that we have ever seen before in all of U.S. history.

John Paul Jackson was shown that someday Mt. Rainier will erupt, and I believe that day is not too far away.

Of course many prophetic voices have seen other volcanoes in the western U.S. erupting as well. If you live anywhere near an active or dormant volcano in the western half of the country, I would strongly encourage you to pray about moving while you still can.

My dream also caused me to reflect on the coming eruption of Mt. Fuji in Japan.

While he was still alive, John Paul Jackson was shown that there will be "three different plumes of smoke or steam" coming from the sides of Mt. Fuji before it finally erupts.

So it won't just happen out of the blue. There will be three warning signs, and when we see those plumes we need to warn everyone that we can.

Unfortunately, most people living in the region will not heed the warnings, and millions will die.

In his vision, John Paul Jackson was absolutely horrified by the scale of the eruption. He described it as "larger than Mount St. Helens", and he saw the city of Tokyo be absolutely destroyed...

"The Volcano blew and smoke and ash came towards the city. It was steam and water and the water was so hot that it melted things. When it hit things, it did not just blow them over but there was a melting that took place. Then a short while later all of the noise became muffled and then quiet, absolute quiet."

In the end, John Paul Jackson said that he was shown that seven million people will die.

If you are able to live long enough, you will see these events happen.

God didn't tell us these things in advance so that we would live in fear. Those that believe what He is telling us and heed the warnings will be able to save themselves from these disasters. Even now, earthquake swarms at Mt. Rainier have been troubling scientists, and I believe that a major eruption is not too far away.

If you live near Mt. Rainier or you know people that do, please do not take these warnings lightly.

As for Mt. Fuji, we know that there will be "three different plumes of smoke or steam" coming from the sides of Mt. Fuji before the really big eruption happens. Once that first plume of smoke starts coming from the volcano, everyone needs to make sure that they are as far from Tokyo as they can possibly get.

I believe that some people will have their lives saved because they will read this book and will choose to heed the warnings.

As our world is greatly shaken and dramatic Earth changes make headlines all over the globe, millions upon millions of people around the world will finally understand that there is still a God in heaven that tells us the end from the beginning. This will result in multitudes being brought into the Kingdom as part of the great and mighty final harvest of the last days.

So even though these seismic events are going to be truly horrific, there is also a redemptive purpose behind them.

God could have picked a random day for "the end" to suddenly come without any warning at all, but He didn't do that.

Instead, there will be a series of great "shakings" that will get progressively worse, and one of the primary purposes of the "shakings" is to turn hearts to God.

So please keep this in mind as you are going through the 7 year apocalypse. It will be an exceedingly difficult time, but it will also be a time when millions upon millions of hardened hearts are finally broken and turned to the one true God that created all things.

God has a purpose for everything that is about to take place, and those that are willing to trust His plan will be used greatly to advance His Kingdom even in the midst of all the chaos that is transpiring all around us.

HYPERINFLATION
AND SHORTAGES

I feel such an urgency to get this book out, because prophecies
are being fulfilled so rapidly right now, and one area where this
is particularly true is in the realm of economics. In *Lost Prophecies Of The Future Of America*, I shared many warnings from
men and women of God all over the world that have been shown
glimpses of the horrific economic collapse that is coming. Many
of them were specifically shown that very painful inflation is
ahead of us, and that is going to make it increasingly difficult for
people to take care of themselves and their families.

For example, John Paul Jackson was shown that at one point
Americans would be spending about 40 percent of their entire
incomes on food and big corporations would be looking to put
armed guards on food trucks because they would become such
prime targets for criminals.

According to the USDA, Americans spent an average of just 9.5
percent of their disposable personal incomes on food in 2019. So
a jump to 40 percent would be quite dramatic, but we are already
starting to move very quickly in that direction. Food prices have
been aggressively moving higher in supermarkets all over the
nation, and what we have experienced so far is just the beginning.

Incredibly, the Book of Revelation warned us that this was coming nearly 2,000 years ago. When the third seal is opened in Revelation chapter 6, we are specifically told that wheat and barley

will become exceedingly expensive...

5 And when he had opened the third seal, I heard the third beast say, Come and see. And I beheld, and lo a black horse; and he that sat on him had a pair of balances in his hand.

6 And I heard a voice in the midst of the four beasts say, A measure of wheat for a penny, and three measures of barley for a penny; and see thou hurt not the oil and the wine.

The COVID pandemic hit global food production and global supply chains really hard, and meanwhile weather patterns all over the planet have continued to go absolutely nuts. Even in the best of years, we really struggle to feed the entire world, and this is definitely not one of the best of years. All around the globe we are witnessing historic droughts, record flooding, giant plagues of locusts and crippling crop failures.

It was inevitable that prices for agricultural commodities would go much higher, and that is precisely what has happened.

In fact, agricultural commodity prices are up by about 50 percent since the middle of 2020, and they just continue to surge even higher.

Of course not everything has been rising at an equal pace. For instance, at one point in 2021 the price of corn was up 142 percent compared to what it was selling for at the same time in 2020.

Here in the United States, corn has become an essential ingredient in hundreds of processed foods. The big food manufacturers put it in our bread, they put it in our soda, they put it in our spaghetti sauce, they put it in the baby formula that we give to our children, and they are constantly coming up with new ways to include it in even more of the packaged foods that we eat.

So an increase in the price of corn is going to affect countless products that average Americans put into their grocery carts on a weekly basis.

But at least the price of corn hasn't gone up as fast as the price of lumber.

At one point, it was being reported that the price of lumber had risen by more than 200 percent over a 12 month period. We have never seen anything like this before, and it has been particularly brutal on the home building industry.

If you can believe it, skyrocketing lumber prices have driven up the average price of a new home in the United States by almost $36,000 over the past 12 months.

A lot of people have simply had to stop construction on new homes that they were building because lumber has become so insanely expensive.

Instead of building a new home, you could go out and try to purchase an existing home, but prices for existing homes are soaring too.

As I write this book, we are witnessing wild bidding wars for properties in desirable rural and suburban communities all across the nation. During the month of March, more than 300 homes in the U.S. sold for more than a million dollars over listing price, and more than 900 homes sold more than half a million dollars over listing price. I never thought that I would see such a thing happen, and it is a sign that the hour is late.

If you are independently wealthy, you still have the opportunity to relocate anywhere that you want, because you can simply outbid everyone else for a particular home that you desire.

But the vast majority of Americans are not independently wealthy, and many of them are discovering that they are now priced out of certain markets.

If you thought that you could wait to relocate until things started getting really crazy, your options are going to be a lot more limited now. You might still be able to relocate success-fully, but you may have to choose an area of the country that was not your first or second or third choice.

So why is inflation starting to spiral out of control?

The answer is actually very simple. When the COVID pandemic came along, our politicians wanted to "save the economy", and so they started to borrow and spend money at a pace that we have never seen before.

They borrowed and spent trillions upon trillions of dollars, and most Americans were absolutely thrilled by the "stimulus checks" that they were getting from the federal government. In fact, one poll discovered that 78 percent of all Americans sup-ported the stimulus checks. A whopping 90 percent of Demo-crats supported the checks, and support among Republicans was at 64 percent. The American people overwhelmingly supported the payments, because they didn't understand the impact that all of this new money would have.

Of course other governments around the globe have also been on massive spending binges. Never before have we seen such a tsu-nami of new money in such a short period of time, and this is starting to cause major problems all over the world.

At the same time, global central banks have been absolutely flooding their respective financial systems with giant moun-tains of cash. Here in the United States, this has helped to fuel the greatest stock market rally in our history, and investors on Wall Street are in a euphoric mood because of the huge gains that they have been seeing.

But there is a great price to pay for all of this "free money".

In Venezuela today, nearly everyone is a "millionaire", but nearly everyone is also living in abject poverty because the money is virtually worthless now.

We are on the exact same path, but most people don't seem to realize this.

Until the people stand up and object, the politicians are just going to continue spending money like mad. The Biden administration has rolled out plans that would mean borrowing and spending trillions more dollars on top of all the spending that we have already done, and many in Congress have expressed enthusiasm for those plans.

And the Federal Reserve continues to pump more cash into the financial system on a daily basis.

What we are doing is completely and utterly insane. You never go "full Weimar", because when you go "full Weimar" it creates horrific inflation and severe shortages.

In this chapter I have already talked about the inflation that we are now witnessing, and so let me talk a bit about shortages.

As I write this chapter, the U.S. economy is currently experiencing shortages of the following to at least some degree...

-Computer Chips
-Pharmaceutical Drugs (the FDA says that 120 drugs are currently in short supply)

-Copper
-Iron Ore
-Steel
-Corn
-Wheat
-Soybeans
-Plastic
-Cardboard
-Used Vehicles
-Lumber
-Building Materials
-Furniture
-Chicken
-Bacon
-Chlorine

To me, the global shortage of computer chips is one of the most serious shortages that we are facing. The head of Intel has warned that it could last into 2023 even under ideal conditions, and that is going to have a huge impact on almost every other industry.

In our time, we have become exceedingly dependent on technology, and our society as it is formulated today simply could not function without it.

Just think about it. Without computer chips, most of our vehicles would not run. Without computer chips, most of our trucks could not transport the products that we buy to the stores. Without computer chips, most of the farm equipment that farmers use to produce our food would be useless.

Just about every industry that you could possibly name uses computers and other equipment that relies on computer chips. Without chips, there are no televisions, phones and laptops. There are chips in the toys that our children play with, and there are chips in the hospital equipment that keeps our terminally ill patients alive. If all of our chips were suddenly taken away, our society would come to a grinding halt and our economy would completely and utterly collapse.

That is why it has been so foolish for us to become so dependent on chip production from Asia.

In 1990, 37 percent of all computer chips were made inside the United States, but at this point that number has dwindled to just 12 percent.

Now that we are in the midst of a full-blown crisis that threatens to last for a number of years, business leaders are pledging to ramp up production here in the U.S., but that will take some time to accomplish.

You can't just plop down factories and start pumping out computer chips. For the most advanced chips, there are more than 1,000 steps in the manufacturing process. Producing chips has gotten to be extremely sophisticated, and we should have never allowed ourselves to fall so far behind.

Of course it isn't just the production of computer chips that we have outsourced.

Did you know that 60 percent of the apple juice sold in the United States now comes from China?

When we were on friendly terms with China, that wasn't a problem, but now relations between our two nations have soured quite dramatically.

And if you have read my last book, you already know where things are eventually heading.

So what is going to happen when the Chinese stop sending us thousands upon thousands of products that they currently make for us?

If you think that the shortages that we are experiencing now are bad, just wait until that happens.

We are living at a time when end times events are really starting to move forward at an extremely rapid pace. So much has happened since I wrote my last book, and I hope to release new books more frequently in the days ahead. As unprecedented apocalyptic events shake our world, millions upon millions of people are going to be searching for answers, and we need to be there to provide those answers.

In just about every area that I addressed in my last book, we are beginning to see prophecies fulfilled. Some of the prophecies are from decades ago, and now is the time when many of those old prophecies are starting to come to pass.

This is an incredibly powerful witnessing tool, because we serve the one true God that has told us the end from the beginning. I believe that multitudes are going to be saved in the years ahead as the Book of Revelation plays out right in front of us.

Sadly, way too many Christian leaders are assuring everyone that peace and prosperity are ahead and that Jesus is not coming back any time soon.

What a tragic mistake.

The economic problems that we have experienced so far are not even worth comparing to the horrors that are coming later. We will see wild inflation and very painful shortages, and beyond that there will be extreme global famines and total economic collapse.

In Matthew 24, Jesus specifically warned us that there will be "famines" in the last days. They will hit the poorest parts of the globe first, but as I detailed in my last book, eventually there will be great famines inside the United States as well.

I know that not everyone is willing to accept this. But if you have eyes to see and ears to hear, then the Lord will confirm in your spirit that what I am telling you is the truth.

Everything is not going to happen overnight, but global events have certainly moved forward quite dramatically since I wrote my last book, and I expect things to accelerate even more in the months ahead.

THE MARK OF THE BEAST

Over the years, very few topics related to Bible prophecy have captured the imagination of the general public the way that the Mark of the Beast has. It has been featured in countless novels, television shows and movies, and yet it remains such a mystery. The Bible doesn't actually go into too much detail about the Mark of the Beast, but what it does have to say is exceedingly important. In this chapter, we are going to look at every single passage in the Book of Revelation that mentions the Mark of the Beast.

During the horrific series of cataclysms that is coming during the first half of the 7 year apocalypse, most of the people that are living in our world today will die. That means that most of the global population will not even make it to the point when the Mark of the Beast is unveiled. But if you are able to stay alive long enough, you will be here for the Mark of the Beast.

Once again, I am not saying this sort of thing for shock value. Rather, I am being very blunt in order to wake people up.

You need to decide right now what you are going to do when confronted with the Mark of the Beast.

Because it won't just be a matter of life and death.

Ultimately, it will be a decision that determines your eternal destiny.

As you will see below, if you choose to take the Mark of the Beast, there is no more hope for you.

Today, so many bizarre theories about the Mark of the Beast are being spread around, and this is causing a tremendous amount of confusion. My hope is that this chapter will help to clarify things. The truth is that we know certain things must happen first before the Mark of the Beast arrives, and when it is finally unveiled there will be absolutely no doubt about what it is.

First of all, there can't be a "Mark of the Beast" until the Beast takes power. As I discuss in another chapter in this book, the Beast does not ascend out of the pit until the fifth angel blows his trumpet in Revelation chapter 9. This occurs in the middle of the Tribulation period, and the Beast will rule for the next three and a half years until Jesus comes back at the end of the Tribulation period.

In fact, we are specifically told that the Beast is given power to make war with the saints for 42 months in the exact same chapter where the Mark of the Beast is first introduced. The following is what Revelation 13:4-18 says in the King James Version...

4 And they worshipped the dragon which gave power unto the beast: and they worshipped the beast, saying, Who is like unto the beast? who is able to make war with him?

5 And there was given unto him a mouth speaking great things and blasphemies; and power was given unto him to continue forty and two months.

6 And he opened his mouth in blasphemy against God, to blaspheme his name, and his tabernacle, and them that dwell in heaven.

7 And it was given unto him to make war with the saints, and to overcome them: and power was given him over all kindreds, and tongues, and nations.

8 And all that dwell upon the earth shall worship him, whose names are not written in the book of life of the Lamb slain from the foundation of the world.

9 If any man have an ear, let him hear.

10 He that leadeth into captivity shall go into captivity: he that killeth with the sword must be killed with the sword. Here is the patience and the faith of the saints.

11 And I beheld another beast coming up out of the earth; and he had two horns like a lamb, and he spake as a dragon.

12 And he exerciseth all the power of the first beast before him, and causeth the earth and them which dwell therein to worship the first beast, whose deadly wound was healed.

13 And he doeth great wonders, so that he maketh fire come down from heaven on the earth in the sight of men,

14 And deceiveth them that dwell on the earth by the means of those miracles which he had power to do in the sight of the beast; saying to them that dwell on the earth, that they should make an image to the beast, which had the wound by a sword, and did live.

15 And he had power to give life unto the image of the beast, that the image of the beast should both speak, and cause that as many as would not worship the image of the beast should be killed.

16 And he causeth all, both small and great, rich and poor, free and bond, to receive a mark in their right hand, or in their foreheads:

17 And that no man might buy or sell, save he that had the mark, or the name of the beast, or the number of his name.

18 Here is wisdom. Let him that hath understanding count the num-

ber of the beast: for it is the number of a man; and his number is Six hundred threescore and six.

In this passage, we are told that the Antichrist is given power to make war with the saints and "overcome them". Various men and women of God that have been given prophetic glimpses into this period of time say that they have seen Christians being hunted down like animals. As it says in verse 10, a great deal of patience and faith will be required from the saints as we go through this period of immense persecution.

All throughout human history there have been times when Christians have been rounded up and executed, but this will top them all.

At the same time or shortly following the rise of the Beast, "another beast" will arise. This other beast is identified as "the false prophet" elsewhere in the Book of Revelation, and he will be capable of performing absolutely incredible miracles.

As the head of the new one world religion, the false prophet will order everyone on the entire globe to worship the Antichrist. Anyone that refuses to worship the Antichrist will be under a death penalty.

In verse 16, we are told that everyone in the world will be required to "receive a mark" in the right hand or in the forehead. Without that mark, you will not be able to buy or sell. In essence, those that refuse will be completely cut off from conducting any form of economic activity at that point.

When I was young, it always puzzled me why the right hand or the forehead would be chosen. But then eventually it occurred to me that the hands and the head are the parts of our bodies that are always visible even when we are fully dressed. When the weather gets really cold we often cover them up, but normally when you see someone in public their hands and head are clearly visible.

In those times, authorities will want to be able to easily identify who has the mark and who doesn't have the mark. Being able to quickly check the hands or the foreheads of everybody will make that quite simple.

When we get to this point, there will be no more sitting on the fence for anyone. Being a Christian will mean forsaking everything, and your old life will be completely over.

Just imagine trying to survive without being able to buy, sell, get a job or have a bank account. Law enforcement authorities will be constantly looking to round up those that haven't taken the mark, and so you will not be able to freely move about in society. If you decide to just cut yourself off from the world and stay inside your home, you take the risk that your neighbors could report on you or that authorities could eventually come knocking on your door to check if you have taken the mark yet.

In the end, there might not be anywhere that is truly safe except for the place of protection in the wilderness that is described in Revelation chapter 12.

Needless to say, there will be countless individuals that will choose the easy path. They will willingly choose to take the Mark of the Beast and worship the Antichrist because they don't want to die.

But in Revelation 14:9-11, we learn that those that choose to take the Mark of the Beast will ultimately have a fate that is far worse than death...

9 And the third angel followed them, saying with a loud voice, If any man worship the beast and his image, and receive his mark in his forehead, or in his hand,

10 The same shall drink of the wine of the wrath of God, which is poured out without mixture into the cup of his indignation; and he shall be tormented with fire and brimstone in the presence of the holy angels, and in the presence of the Lamb:

11 And the smoke of their torment ascendeth up for ever and ever: and they have no rest day nor night, who worship the beast and his image, and whosoever receiveth the mark of his name.

No matter what, do not take the Mark of the Beast.

Some people may be tempted to think that "God will forgive them" for taking the Mark of the Beast, but Revelation 14 makes it clear that this is not the case.

In fact, men and women of God that have been given glimpses into this period of time say that they have been shown that those that take the Mark of the Beast appear to no longer have free will.

In other words, you may not even be capable of asking God to forgive you once you have taken the Mark of the Beast.

But it will be so tempting to take the Mark of the Beast when faced with imminent death.

That is why you need to make your decision now. Vast numbers of Christians will be executed for their faith, but in the end it will all be worth it. To me, Revelation 15:2 is such an encouraging verse...

And I saw as it were a sea of glass mingled with fire: and them that had gotten the victory over the beast, and over his image, and over his mark, and over the number of his name, stand on the sea of glass, having the harps of God.

You can have victory over the Antichrist and the Mark of the Beast too. But in order to do that, you must be ready to lay down your life for Jesus.

In Revelation 16, the seven vials of God's wrath are poured out upon the Earth just prior to the time when Jesus returns with His armies to defeat the Antichrist, and the pouring out of the first vial results in "grievous" sores appearing on those that have taken the Mark of the Beast. This is what Revelation 16:2 says...

And the first went, and poured out his vial upon the earth; and there fell a noisome and grievous sore upon the men which had the mark of the beast, and upon them which worshipped his image.

Six more vials of wrath are subsequently poured out upon the Earth, and then Jesus returns with His saints in Revelation 19. The Beast and the false prophet are captured, and in Revelation 19:20 we are told that those two are thrown directly into the lake of fire...

And the beast was taken, and with him the false prophet that wrought miracles before him, with which he deceived them that had received the mark of the beast, and them that worshipped his image. These both were cast alive into a lake of fire burning with brimstone.

On the other hand, those that have been faithful to Christ and have refused the Mark of the Beast reign with Christ for 1,000 years as it tells us in Revelation 20:4...

And I saw thrones, and they sat upon them, and judgment was given unto them: and I saw the souls of them that were beheaded for the witness of Jesus, and for the word of God, and which had not worshipped the beast, neither his image, neither had received his mark upon their foreheads, or in their hands; and they lived and reigned with Christ a thousand years.

So there you have it.

Those are all the passages where the Mark of the Beast is mentioned.

Many have been fascinated by the mention of beheading in Revelation 20:4, and quite a few prophetic voices have specifically been shown that this is a method of execution that will be used on those that refuse the Mark.

I understand that the idea of facing such a moment is extremely unpleasant.

But God would not allow you to go through such a trial if He didn't think that you could handle it.

If we are faithful to the point of death, we will inherit a crown of life.

So don't be afraid.

God will give us the grace and strength that we need exactly when we need it.

When Jesus died on the cross, He gave His very best for you.

Are you willing to give your very best for Him?

The time when all of this will be happening is rapidly approaching, and that is why our churches desperately need to be preparing believers to face persecution, suffering and martyrdom.

Unfortunately, way too many Christian leaders are preaching messages of success and prosperity these days, and most of our churches are not even talking about the end times at all.

END TIMES UFO
DECEPTION

We live at a time when interest in UFOs and aliens is at an all-time high, and many are concerned that this could be setting the stage for a colossal end times deception. According to a Gallup survey that was conducted a couple of years ago, 16 percent of all Americans claim to have seen a UFO. That is an alarmingly high number, but of even greater concern is the large number of Americans that claim that they have either been abducted by aliens or have had a close personal encounter with them. In the old days, it was easier to dismiss such reports as coming from "crazy people", but over the years the number of people reporting such experiences has continued to grow.

It is not a coincidence that a large proportion of the people that have reported encounters with alien beings are also involved with occult or New Age practices. For a very long time, Christian researchers such as L.A. Marzulli, Steve Quayle and Tom Horn have been documenting the links between the UFO phenomenon and dark spiritual forces. Aliens often masquerade as "beings of light" that have come from another world to help humanity, but it has been impossible for them to hide their deeply insidious agenda.

Much of the time, communication between "aliens" and humans turns in a spiritual direction very quickly. There is a lot of inconsistency in the claims that these "aliens" are making, and that is because they are lying through their teeth, but what is very clear is that they absolutely hate Christians and the Christian faith. A future spiritual "awakening" for humanity is a theme that often comes up when New Agers and occultists communicate with "aliens", and of course those that are into occult or New Age practices love to hear that.

And there have been numerous reports that indicate that these "aliens" really, really do not like the name of Jesus. In fact, there are quite a few reports of them fleeing when commanded to do so in the name of Jesus.

So if you ever find yourself confronted by beings that you cannot identify, command them to depart in the name of Jesus just like you would do if confronted by demonic entities.

And of course the reason why "alien beings" behave the same way is because they are straight from the kingdom of darkness.

Unfortunately, I believe that the stage is now being set for an end times UFO deception of epic proportions.

During a recent interview on the Ezra Klein Show, Barack Obama was asked what he knew about UFOs and aliens. He made a few vague statements that made it very clear that he believes that they are real, and then he said something that absolutely floored me.

According to Obama, he believes that UFOs could cause "new religions" to come into existence...

"New religions would pop up. And who knows what kind of arguments we get into. We're good at manufacturing arguments for each other."

What a statement to make.

Why would Barack Obama come to the conclusion that the UFO

phenomenon could cause some sort of dramatic spiritual shift for humanity?

Does he know things that he is not telling us?

I believe that he does.

In the old days, U.S. government agencies would go to great lengths to deny that UFOs and aliens existed. Anyone that was too vocal about such things was marginalized, and those that showed that they were effective in getting the truth out were likely to get a visit from shadowy government agents.

But now everything has changed.

Here in 2021, the government is openly admitting that the UFO phenomenon is real. Members of Congress such as Senator Marco Rubio regularly appear on television discussing the topic, and former Senate majority leader Harry Reid recently wrote a very long article about what he knows that was published in the New York Times.

Even 60 Minutes has now aired a report about UFO sightings. In fact, they interviewed a former U.S. Navy pilot named Ryan Graves that said that his squadron encountered UFOs "every day for at least a couple years" during one stretch.

So why is this happening all of a sudden?

Instead of trying to shut down discussions about this subject, now the federal government and the mainstream media can't stop talking about it.

Could it be possible that they are trying to mentally prepare us for something?

Today, UFO sightings are being reported by ordinary citizens at a rate that we have never seen before. According to the New York Times, over 7,200 different sightings were reported to the National UFO Reporting Center in 2020, and that represented an increase of "about 1,000" from 2019.

In their article about this, the New York Times blamed the COVID pandemic for the increase in UFO sightings. The article suggested that sightings were probably up because people had more free time on their hands and spent more time looking up into the sky while the pandemic was raging.

That theory seemed somewhat reasonable to me when I first read that article, but I decided to dig deeper.

So I looked up the numbers for the previous year, and what I discovered astounded me.

It turns out that the increase in UFO sightings in 2019 was even larger than the increase in UFO sightings that we witnessed in 2020.

According to the National UFO Reporting Center, 5,971 UFO sightings were reported in 2019, and that was way up from just 3,395 in 2018.

Needless to say, we can't blame that even larger increase on the COVID pandemic, because there was no COVID pandemic in 2019.

So why did the number of UFO sightings rise so dramatically in 2019?

And why did that number go even higher in 2020?

I think that those are very important questions.

Overall, the number of UFO sightings has more than doubled in the past two years.

And this has happened at a time when our politicians, U.S. government agencies and the mainstream media suddenly seem quite eager to talk about UFOs.

All of this seems rather odd, doesn't it?

I believe that this is going to become a bigger story over time, and Christians are going to need to have answers for a general public that is going to be very, very confused.

I also believe that UFO and "alien" activity will continue to increase, but the "big reveal" is not going to happen just yet.

In a previous chapter in this book, I discussed how Revelation chapter 9 describes "an invasion of Earth by supernatural forces from the bottomless pit". I would like for you to read Revelation chapter 9 again now that you have had a chance to digest the information that I have shared in this chapter...

And the fifth angel sounded, and I saw a star fall from heaven unto the earth: and to him was given the key of the bottomless pit.

2 And he opened the bottomless pit; and there arose a smoke out of the pit, as the smoke of a great furnace; and the sun and the air were darkened by reason of the smoke of the pit.

3 And there came out of the smoke locusts upon the earth: and unto them was given power, as the scorpions of the earth have power.

4 And it was commanded them that they should not hurt the grass of the earth, neither any green thing, neither any tree; but only those men which have not the seal of God in their foreheads.

5 And to them it was given that they should not kill them, but that they should be tormented five months: and their torment was as the torment of a scorpion, when he striketh a man.

6 And in those days shall men seek death, and shall not find it; and shall desire to die, and death shall flee from them.

7 And the shapes of the locusts were like unto horses prepared unto battle; and on their heads were as it were crowns like gold, and their faces were as the faces of men.

8 And they had hair as the hair of women, and their teeth were as the teeth of lions.

9 And they had breastplates, as it were breastplates of iron; and the sound of their wings was as the sound of chariots of many horses running to battle.

10 And they had tails like unto scorpions, and there were stings in their tails: and their power was to hurt men five months.

11 And they had a king over them, which is the angel of the bottomless pit, whose name in the Hebrew tongue is Abaddon, but in the Greek tongue hath his name Apollyon.

12 One woe is past; and, behold, there come two woes more hereafter.

13 And the sixth angel sounded, and I heard a voice from the four horns of the golden altar which is before God,

14 Saying to the sixth angel which had the trumpet, Loose the four angels which are bound in the great river Euphrates.

15 And the four angels were loosed, which were prepared for an hour, and a day, and a month, and a year, for to slay the third part of men.

16 And the number of the army of the horsemen were two hundred thousand thousand: and I heard the number of them.

17 And thus I saw the horses in the vision, and them that sat on them, having breastplates of fire, and of jacinth, and brimstone: and the heads of the horses were as the heads of lions; and out of their mouths issued fire and smoke and brimstone.

18 By these three was the third part of men killed, by the fire, and by the smoke, and by the brimstone, which issued out of their mouths.

19 For their power is in their mouth, and in their tails: for their tails were like unto serpents, and had heads, and with them they do hurt.

20 And the rest of the men which were not killed by these plagues yet repented not of the works of their hands, that they should not worship devils, and idols of gold, and silver, and brass, and stone, and of wood: which neither can see, nor hear, nor walk:

21 Neither repented they of their murders, nor of their sorceries, nor of their fornication, nor of their thefts.

The more I read this, the more I am convinced that this is literally a demonic invasion of our planet by forces that are led by the Antichrist.

It will be wilder than anything that the best science fiction writers in Hollywood could ever come up with, and there will be so much confusion.

The vast majority of the people still alive at that time won't understand who the invaders are or where they have come from.

I believe that this is where the "alien deception" comes in. The invading forces will almost certainly be identified as "aliens", and most of those that survive the invasion will eagerly submit to the new one world government and the new one world religion that their new alien overlords have brought with them.

The Antichrist will be heralded as the "Messiah" that so many world religions have been anticipating, and he will promise a new era of global peace and prosperity now that he has utterly crushed the "closed-minded individuals" that resisted him.

When the times comes, we won't have to guess the identity of the Antichrist.

His arrival will be a spectacular event, and it will be impossible to miss him.

The Mark of the Beast will be instituted after his arrival, and that will be impossible to miss too.

But even though there will be no denying what the Mark of the Beast is, vast multitudes will take it anyway because they don't want to die.

It is hard to imagine what our world will look like during this time. So much is going to change during the first half of the 7 year apocalypse, and the horrors of that three and a half year period will set the stage for the rise of the Beast and his invading armies.

I understand that some of the opinions I have expressed in this chapter are controversial. If you find yourself disagreeing with me on some things, that is okay.

The closer that we get to the actual events of the 7 year apocalypse, the clearer that things will become for all of us.

But let there be absolutely no doubt about one thing. The Beast is definitely coming, and once he arrives our world will be thrown into a state of complete and utter chaos.

THE NAFTALI BENNETT DREAM

This is another dream that I was originally not going to share with anyone. It wasn't a long dream, but I believe that it was extremely significant.

On the morning of May 30th, 2021 I had a very vivid dream which really surprised me. In the dream, I repeatedly saw Israeli politician Naftali Bennett, and it was repeatedly communicated to me that he would be the next prime minister of Israel.

This was very strange, because Benjamin Netanyahu's party had received the most votes by far in the last election, and Netanyahu had been the prime minister in Israel for ages. Bennett's Yamina party had only won 7 seats in the election, and nobody had ever served as prime minister in Israel after his party had won so few seats.

When I woke up later that morning, I checked the news and I saw that it was filled with headlines about a potential deal between Naftali Bennett and Yair Lapid. There was still much that needed to be negotiated, but it was being reported that Bennett and Lapid would take turns being prime minister, with Bennett going first.

This caused a huge uproar in Israel, because prior to the election Bennett had pledged that he would never make a deal that would lead to Lapid becoming the prime minister. Many conservative Israelis felt like Bennett was betraying them, because now Netanyahu would be out.

Unfortunately, Bennett did not back down, and his deal with Lapid turned Israeli politics completely upside down.

Bennett has become the prime minister just like I saw in my dream, and I believe that this sets the stage for even more prophetic fulfillments.

While he was still alive, Henry Gruver reportedly gave us the following prophetic warning: "When Israel sends troops into Gaza, it will be a sign the Middle East War has started."

During the fighting between Israel and Hamas in May, Israeli troops went right up to the border and fired into Gaza, but they never actually crossed it. Myself and others were wondering if that would be the moment when Gruver's prophecy would be fulfilled, but it wasn't.

As I write this chapter, the ceasefire that Israel and Hamas ultimately agreed to is still holding, but that could change at literally any moment. By the time you are reading this book, a major war may have broken out.

The use of the phrase "the Middle East War" in Gruver's prophecy seems to imply that the conflict that he is referring to will include more parties that just Israel and Hamas.

Could Hezbollah decide to attack Israel from the north while the IDF is focused on Hamas in the south?

And could such a conflict be the thing that sparks a major war between Israel and Iran?

I don't have the answers to those questions as I write this chapter, but eventually we will get those answers as events move forward.

In the aftermath of the coming Middle East war, the entire globe will be crying out for peace, and it is at that time that I believe there will be some sort of a "permanent" deal dividing the land of Israel into two states.

For a number of years, there were two major factors holding back negotiations that would lead to a "two state solution".

First of all, the Palestinians were never going to do a deal while Donald Trump was in the White House, but now he is out of the picture.

Secondly, there is no way that Israel will ever agree to a "two state solution" as long as Hamas is running Gaza. But if Israel destroys Hamas during a future military conflict, that would make it possible for all of the Palestinians to be united under the leadership of Mahmoud Abbas, and negotiations regarding the establishment of a "two state solution" could move forward.

In *Lost Prophecies Of The Future Of America*, I shared testimonies from a large number of men and women of God that have been shown that someday the U.S. government will be involved in formally dividing the land of Israel. As a result, God is literally going to rip the North American continent in half along the New Madrid fault.

The Biden administration has been very vocal about the fact that it sees a "two state solution" as the key to lasting peace in the Middle East, and once the coming Middle East war is over the Biden administration will undoubtedly work extremely hard to make a "two state solution" a reality.

So to summarize, I believe that three major events are coming, and all of the players are now in place.

First, I believe that a major Middle East war will start when Israel sends troops into Gaza. Benjamin Netanyahu was always very hesitant to do such a thing, but Naftali Bennett is younger and more aggressive, and I believe that he could be the one that sends Israeli troops across the border to deal with the Hamas problem once and for all. We don't know for sure that it will be Bennett, but he has always wanted Netanyahu to be far more aggressive with Hamas, and now he finally has the chance to run things his way.

Secondly, I believe that the Biden administration (or the Harris administration) will push extremely hard for a "two state solution" after the coming Middle East war ends. With the way that Joe Biden is deteriorating physically, he may not make it to that point and Kamala Harris may need to take over for him. In any event, I believe that a Democrat will probably be in the White House when the land of Israel is formally divided.

Following the division of the land of Israel, the United States will literally be physically divided in two along the New Madrid fault zone.

As I have written elsewhere, we don't know how soon the great New Madrid earthquake will happen after a two state solution is implemented. It could be days, it could be weeks, it could be months, or it could be years.

We just don't know.

But what we do know is that it will happen. For much more on this, please read my previous book entitled *Lost Prophecies Of The Future Of America*.

Sadly, even though we were warned about all of these things decades in advance, our leaders in Washington are not listening to the warnings and they intend to push very hard for a "two state solution" in the Middle East.

So if you live anywhere near the New Madrid fault zone, you are going to have some very important decisions to make. Once you hear that a "two state solution" is being negotiated, you will need to decide whether you want to stay or leave.

Personally, I wouldn't want to be anywhere around the New Madrid fault zone when the U.S. is finally ripped in two, because the death and destruction will be absolutely unimaginable.

The good news is that large numbers of people will hear warnings about what is going to happen and will save their lives by getting out of the region in advance.

This book and others like it will save countless lives in the years ahead, but even more importantly they will play a role in saving countless souls as well.

REVIVAL

I know that there is a lot of bad news in this book.

When the reality of what is about to happen to this planet sinks in and you understand that everything that I am telling you is real, it can be difficult to deal with emotionally.

We have become a radically "me focused" society, and most of us are deeply obsessed with ourselves. As our world is shaken and the grandiose plans that most people had for their own lives are shattered, many will not be able to handle it and we will witness a societal temper tantrum to end all temper tantrums.

If your life is all about you, the times that are ahead are likely to drive you mad.

But if your life has been surrendered to God and you are living for His Kingdom, the days that are coming can be incredibly exciting if you embrace what He is trying to do.

For years, I have been publicly proclaiming that we will soon experience the greatest move of God and the greatest harvest of souls that the world has ever seen. But because most of our churches are so dead and because most of them never talk about such things, many believers don't even have any idea what that could look like.

Here in the United States, there hasn't been a widespread move of God in decades. To me, the last widespread move of God was probably the "Jesus people movement" of the 1970s. Since that time there have been small regional outbreaks of revival, but nothing nationwide.

I have been praying for revival since 1988. That was my first year as an undergraduate at the University of Virginia, and I really hope that some of those that knew me then are reading this book. I remember gathering almost every night with close friends to pray for revival. In those days, we thought that it would come a lot sooner, but after all this time we are still waiting.

Even though we are still waiting for a widespread move of God, there is no denying that God has been working mightily in these end times. The Remnant of the last days is rising, and I know this because I interact with members of that Remnant that are located all over the world.

And we know exactly what the Remnant will look like in the last days, because the Bible clearly tells us what it will look like. Revelation 12:17 tells us the following...

17 And the dragon was wroth with the woman, and went to make war with the remnant of her seed, which keep the commandments of God, and have the testimony of Jesus Christ.

In case you missed it the first time, the Remnant of the last days is defined again in Revelation 14:12...

12 Here is the patience of the saints: here are they that keep the commandments of God, and the faith of Jesus.

When God takes the time to tell us something more than once, it is imperative for us to pay attention.

Unfortunately, most churches today don't want anything to do with the commandments of God, and most of them have put the testimony of Jesus Christ on the back burner.

All over the world, God is raising up a Remnant in these last days that will keep His commandments, that will preach His gospel to the whole world and bring in the greatest harvest of souls in all of human history, and that will move in all the fruit, all the gifts and all the power of the Holy Spirit like we haven't seen since the Book of Acts.

If there is something in that statement that offends you, just keep doing things the way that you have been doing them all this time, and you will continue to get the same results.

But if you want to be on the cutting edge of what God is doing in these last days, I would encourage you to embrace what the Bible has to say about the Remnant of the last days.

We don't have to play a guessing game when it comes to the last move of God before the return of Jesus, because God has already told us what it will look like.

Those that are part of this Remnant will be so on fire for God that they will not hesitate to lay down their lives for Jesus if that becomes necessary. In Revelation 15, we find those that have "gotten the victory over the beast, and over his image, and over his mark" standing on the sea of glass giving praise to God...

And I saw another sign in heaven, great and marvellous, seven angels having the seven last plagues; for in them is filled up the wrath of God.

2 And I saw as it were a sea of glass mingled with fire: and them that had gotten the victory over the beast, and over his image, and over his mark, and over the number of his name, stand on the sea of glass, having the harps of God.

3 And they sing the song of Moses the servant of God, and the song of the Lamb, saying, Great and marvellous are thy works, Lord God Almighty; just and true are thy ways, thou King of saints.

4 Who shall not fear thee, O Lord, and glorify thy name? for thou only art holy: for all nations shall come and worship before thee; for thy judgments are made manifest.

If you stay true to Jesus, even in the face of death, you will be victorious in the end.

As the Apostle Paul said in Philippians 1:21, "to live is Christ, and to die is gain".

Throughout the Book of Revelation, we find promises for those that are "overcomers". On our own we can do nothing, but with God all things are possible. During the difficult times that are coming, here are some specific promises to cling to very tightly...

Revelation 2:7 - He that hath an ear, let him hear what the Spirit saith unto the churches; To him that overcometh will I give to eat of the tree of life, which is in the midst of the paradise of God.

Revelation 2:11 - He that hath an ear, let him hear what the Spirit saith unto the churches; He that overcometh shall not be hurt of the second death.

Revelation 2:17 - He that hath an ear, let him hear what the Spirit saith unto the churches; To him that overcometh will I give to eat of the hidden manna, and will give him a white stone, and in the stone a new name written, which no man knoweth saving he that receiveth it.

Revelation 2:26 - And he that overcometh, and keepeth my works unto the end, to him will I give power over the nations:

157

Revelation 3:5 - He that overcometh, the same shall be clothed in white raiment; and I will not blot out his name out of the book of life, but I will confess his name before my Father, and before his angels.

Revelation 3:12 - Him that overcometh will I make a pillar in the temple of my God, and he shall go no more out: and I will write upon him the name of my God, and the name of the city of my God, which is new Jerusalem, which cometh down out of heaven from my God: and I will write upon him my new name.

Revelation 3:21 - To him that overcometh will I grant to sit with me in my throne, even as I also overcame, and am set down with my Father in his throne.

Revelation 21:7 - He that overcometh shall inherit all things; and I will be his God, and he shall be my son.

You can be one of those "overcomers", but you have got to be willing to surrender all to the Lord Jesus Christ.

Nothing compares to living for God. All of the money in the entire world is not even worth comparing to the surpassing greatness of knowing Him and serving His kingdom. But so many people out there are pushing God away for far, far less.

When your life is finally over, what are you going to have to show for it?

Will your bank account be your legacy?

Will you have spent your prime years serving some heartless organization that doesn't even care about you?

When you look back, will you be able to say that you truly made a difference in the lives of others?

The greatest thing that you could ever do for someone else is to help that person find eternal life through Jesus Christ.

If you can grasp that simple truth, it will set your heart totally on fire.

Human history has been forged in the context of an epic cosmic battle between good and evil. Now that battle is getting ready to come to a grand crescendo, and we get to be here for that.

There are literally billions of souls hanging in the balance, and time is running out.

So wake up and stop obsessing over things that don't really matter.

In Daniel chapter 12, the resurrection of believers is described, and we are told that those that "turn many to righteousness" will shine like the stars...

2 And many of them that sleep in the dust of the earth shall awake, some to everlasting life, and some to shame and everlasting contempt.

3 And they that be wise shall shine as the brightness of the firmament; and they that turn many to righteousness as the stars for ever and ever.

No matter what your life has been like up to this point, it is not too late for you.

Surrender your life to Jesus and start serving Him with everything that you have got.

It isn't an accident that you are reading this book. You were drawn to this book for a reason, and for some of you this moment could represent a major turning point.

Are you ready for what God has planned for the next chapter of your life?

For my wife and I, we believe that the greatest chapters of our lives are still ahead of us. We desperately want to be part of the great move of God that will happen in these end times, and we desperately want to be on the front lines of the great harvest of souls that is coming.

So please pray that the Lord would give us what we need in order to do that.

There is no feeling in the world like being consumed with a passion for God and a passion for building His Kingdom.

But this world literally has millions of different ways to distract you from what is really important.

For those that have been slumbering, it is time to awaken, because the greatest move of God the world has ever seen will soon be here. I have prayed for it surrounded by other young believers at the Rock House at the University of Virginia, I have prayed for it on the streets of Moscow, Russia as I shared the gospel with lost Russians, I have prayed for it on the sandy shores of Daytona Beach, I have prayed for it in front of the White House in Washington D.C., I have prayed for it among spiritual giants at Morningside, and I have prayed for it walking on majestic mountain paths under the endless skies of the Great Northwest.

A vast multitude of other Remnant believers has been praying as well. All over the world, small fires are burning, and we shall join together to set this world on fire for our Lord and Savior Jesus Christ.

Don't miss out on what God is going to do.

God doesn't want you to waste your life. He wants you to be part of something that is far bigger than most people can even imagine, but it is up to you to embrace that plan.

In life, everyone gets knocked down at some point.

But those that refuse to stay down are the ones that end up being victorious.

Don't let your past keep you from the future that you are supposed to have.

God can make a way where there seems to be no way.

If you will give everything to Him, He will take the broken pieces of your life and turn them into a beautiful thing, and He will help you to live a life that really matters.

ONE THING ALMOST EVERYONE MISSES

There is a major theme that runs all throughout the Book of Revelation, and yet almost everyone misses it. When books or movies are made about the Book of Revelation, they tend to focus on topics like the rapture and the Antichrist, but the word "rapture" is not actually in the Book of Revelation and neither is the word "Antichrist". But the words "repent" and "repented" are collectively used 12 different times.

From the very beginning to the very end, the Book of Revelation represents God's last call for humanity to return to Him.

As I have discussed previously, God could have picked some random day to be "the end", and He could have had it come without any warning whatsoever.

But He hasn't done that.

Instead, there will be a very long series of "shakings" over the course of the 7 year apocalypse, and each shaking is intended to be a wake up call. There will be more signs, wonders and miracles during the 7 year apocalypse than during any other 7 year period in all of human history up to this point, and I believe that multitudes upon multitudes will be saved as a result of those signs, wonders and miracles.

Today, hearts are more hardened than they have ever been in my entire lifetime. Particularly in the western world, the vast majority of the population does not want to hear anyone preaching to them about God and His ways.

If "the end" came at this moment, the number of people that would be lost eternally would be unimaginable.

Fortunately, God has a plan.

During the first half of the 7 year apocalypse, God is going to lift His hand of protection and show the entire world the end result of humanity's prideful attempts to run things their way.

During the second half of the 7 year apocalypse, God is going to give Satan and the Antichrist the opportunity to run things, and the folly of following the forces of darkness will be completely and utterly exposed.

Throughout all seven years, there will be a series of specific events that were prophesied way in advance. Every time one of those prophetic events takes place, it will be an opportunity for the entire population of the globe to wake up and recognize their need for the God that created them.

In our day and time, most people have an extreme aversion to being told that they are wrong about anything, and the word "repent" is so offensive to most people that even most churches never use that word anymore.

But "repent" is not a bad word. It simply means to change direction. Even though we don't deserve it, God has been patiently calling us to turn from our exceedingly wicked ways and start following Him.

Earlier, I mentioned that the words "repent" and "repented" are collectively used 12 different times in the Book of Revelation. Here are the ten verses where those 12 instances occur...

Revelation 2:5 - Remember therefore from whence thou art fallen, and repent, and do the first works; or else I will come unto thee quickly, and will remove thy candlestick out of his place, except thou repent.

Revelation 2:16 - Repent; or else I will come unto thee quickly, and will fight against them with the sword of my mouth.

Revelation 2:21 - And I gave her space to repent of her fornication; and she repented not.

Revelation 2:22 - Behold, I will cast her into a bed, and them that commit adultery with her into great tribulation, except they repent of their deeds.

Revelation 3:3 - Remember therefore how thou hast received and heard, and hold fast, and repent. If therefore thou shalt not watch, I will come on thee as a thief, and thou shalt not know what hour I will come upon thee.

Revelation 3:19 - As many as I love, I rebuke and chasten: be zealous therefore, and repent.

Revelation 9:20 - And the rest of the men which were not killed by these plagues yet repented not of the works of their hands, that they should not worship devils, and idols of gold, and silver, and brass, and stone, and of wood: which neither can see, nor hear, nor walk:

Revelation 9:21 - Neither repented they of their murders, nor of their sorceries, nor of their fornication, nor of their thefts.

Revelation 16:9 - And men were scorched with great heat, and blasphemed the name of God, which hath power over these plagues: and they repented not to give him glory.

Revelation 16:11 - And blasphemed the God of heaven because of their pains and their sores, and repented not of their deeds.

The first six verses listed above come from the letters to the seven churches in Revelation chapter 2 and Revelation chapter 3.

So much of the time we think that it is "the world" that needs to repent, and they do, but the truth is that great repentance is needed inside "the church" as well.

When you look at the numbers, "the church" is nearly as sinful as "the world" at this point. The percentage of Christians that watches pornography is about the same as the percentage of the general population that watches pornography. The divorce rate among Christians is also very similar to the divorce rate in the general population. In staggering numbers, Christians are getting sexually-transmitted diseases, getting pregnant outside of marriage, and having abortions.

And that is just the tip of the iceberg. Drug abuse is rampant in our churches. Child abuse is rampant in our churches. Adultery is rampant in our churches. Dishonesty, greed and theft are rampant in our churches.

On top of everything else, there is a tremendous amount of occult activity that is going on in Christian circles right now.

Just about every form of wickedness that you can possibly imagine is exploding in our society today, and just about every form of wickedness that you can possibly imagine is exploding in our churches today.

From the very beginning, God has given humanity choices. He doesn't force anyone to choose what is right, and He doesn't force anyone to follow Him.

Of course there are consequences for the choices that we make. Throughout the Scriptures, we see great blessings for those that choose to follow God and keep His commandments, and we see very painful consequences for those that reject God and want nothing to do with His ways. This is even true in the very last chapter of the Bible. This is what Revelation 22:14-15 tells us in the King James Version...

14 Blessed are they that do his commandments, that they may have right to the tree of life, and may enter in through the gates into the city.

15 For without are dogs, and sorcerers, and whoremongers, and murderers, and idolaters, and whosoever loveth and maketh a lie.

What part of "blessed are they that do his commandments" is so hard to understand?

God has given us instructions about how to live because He loves us. Those that choose to renounce those instructions do so at their own peril.

Needless to say, verse 15 is not talking about literal "dogs". The Greek word that is translated as "dogs" is "kyon", and according to Blue Letter Bible it can be used as a metaphor for "a man of impure mind" or "an impudent man".

Also, in verse 15 many of the specific sins that are plaguing our society today are listed. Sexual immorality is condemned ("whoremongers"), false religion is condemned (idolaters), and occult activity and witchcraft are condemned (sorcerers).

In addition, it is quite noteworthy that "murderers" made the list in verse 15, because since Roe v. Wade was decided in 1973 more than 1.5 billion babies have been murdered worldwide.

Of course we should not forget the last sin on the list. The average American watches 238 minutes of television a day, and just about all of our "news" and "entertainment" is filled with endless lies. If you allow anyone to pump that much "programming" into your mind every day, it is going to radically alter how you view the world.

In our society, the truth about so many things has been buried under layer after layer of lies. If you go digging for the truth, especially about controversial topics, you are likely to be labeled a "conspiracy theorist" because you aren't agreeing with the established narratives that the global elite are pushing.

But the truth about most things is out there, and you can find it if you are willing to seek it out.

Following the warnings in verses 14 and 15, we find one more invitation to turn to God as the final chapter in the entire Bible comes to a conclusion...

16 I Jesus have sent mine angel to testify unto you these things in the churches. I am the root and the offspring of David, and the bright and morning star.

17 And the Spirit and the bride say, Come. And let him that heareth say, Come. And let him that is athirst come. And whosoever will, let him take the water of life freely.

18 For I testify unto every man that heareth the words of the prophecy of this book, If any man shall add unto these things, God shall add unto him the plagues that are written in this book:

19 And if any man shall take away from the words of the book of this prophecy, God shall take away his part out of the book of life, and out of the holy city, and from the things which are written in this book.

20 He which testifieth these things saith, Surely I come quickly. Amen. Even so, come, Lord Jesus.

21 The grace of our Lord Jesus Christ be with you all. Amen.

What a powerful way to end the Book of Revelation.

Jesus Christ is coming back, and we get to be alive during the time just before it happens.

For those of us that know Jesus, the imminency of His return gives us great hope.

But if you don't know Jesus yet, you are currently facing a future with no hope.

In the next chapter, I am going to explain how you can surrender your life to God and enter into a personal relationship with Jesus Christ. It is the most important decision that you could ever make, because it has eternal consequences.

Of course the next chapter is not just for non-believers. There are millions upon millions of backslidden Christians that have fallen away from God in recent years, and now is the time for them to rededicate their lives to Jesus and to return to the Lord with all of their hearts.

If you are in that category, the next chapter is for you too.

God created you, He loves you, and He wants you to spend eternity with Him.

But the choice is up to you.

Choose wisely.

THE MOST IMPORTANT THING

I realize that many of the things that I have shared in this book are difficult to hear.

We really are heading into the most nightmarish period of time in all of human history, and billions of people are going to die.

In fact, the vast majority of the current population of the planet will be dead by the time we get to the end of the 7 year apocalypse.

Virtually everything that people have built their lives around in this world is going to be destroyed. Even if you are fortunate enough to survive all of the cataclysmic events that are coming, most of those that you once knew will be dead, and just trying to survive from day to day will be exceedingly difficult.

Over the years, I have had individuals that don't know Jesus ask me how they can have hope during the times that we are moving into.

In response, I am very honest with them.

I don't know how anyone can possibly have any hope for the future without Jesus.

The great cosmic battle between good and evil is about to reach a grand crescendo, and Jesus is coming back to this planet to set everything right. The forces of evil will be defeated, and Jesus will reign from Jerusalem for 1,000 years. When the 1,000 years are over, Satan will be released one last time and he will attempt one last futile rebellion.

Once that rebellion is crushed, all things will be made new, and we will be with our King forever.

If you don't want anything to do with Jesus, there is no hope for you in that scenario.

The good news is that you can give your life to Jesus right now.

God loves you with a love that is so overwhelming that none of us could ever come up with words that are sufficient to describe it. God created you, He placed you at this specific moment in human history, and He has been watching over you throughout your entire life. He desperately wants a relationship with you, but any relationship is a two way street.

He is reaching out to you, but you have got to be willing to reach out to Him.

Unfortunately, throughout most of recorded history humanity has deeply rejected God and His ways, and that is especially true today. Most of us have eagerly embraced darkness, and just about every form of evil that you can possibly imagine is absolutely exploding in our society today. As a result, our world is full of pain, suffering, violence, depression, despair, anger, frustration and wickedness. Even formerly Christian nations such as the United States have completely abandoned God, and the consequences for doing that have been extremely bitter.

From the very beginning, God has always given us choices. He wants us to choose what is right and to follow His ways, but He does not force anyone to do so.

And we don't have to guess what is right and what is wrong, because He has given us very specific instructions in the Scriptures. Perhaps the best known list of those instructions is the "Ten Commandments", and we find the "Ten Commandments" spelled out for us in Exodus chapter 20...

3 Thou shalt have no other gods before me.

4 Thou shalt not make unto thee any graven image, or any likeness of any thing that is in heaven above, or that is in the earth beneath, or that is in the water under the earth.

5 Thou shalt not bow down thyself to them, nor serve them: for I the Lord thy God am a jealous God, visiting the iniquity of the fathers upon the children unto the third and fourth generation of them that hate me;

6 And shewing mercy unto thousands of them that love me, and keep my commandments.

7 Thou shalt not take the name of the Lord thy God in vain; for the Lord will not hold him guiltless that taketh his name in vain.

8 Remember the sabbath day, to keep it holy.

9 Six days shalt thou labour, and do all thy work:

10 But the seventh day is the sabbath of the Lord thy God: in it thou shalt not do any work, thou, nor thy son, nor thy daughter, thy man-servant, nor thy maidservant, nor thy cattle, nor thy stranger that is within thy gates:

11 For in six days the Lord made heaven and earth, the sea, and all that in them is, and rested the seventh day: wherefore the Lord blessed the sabbath day, and hallowed it.

12 Honour thy father and thy mother: that thy days may be long upon the land which the Lord thy God giveth thee.

13 Thou shalt not kill.

14 Thou shalt not commit adultery.

15 Thou shalt not steal.

16 Thou shalt not bear false witness against thy neighbour.

17 Thou shalt not covet thy neighbour's house, thou shalt not covet thy neighbour's wife, nor his manservant, nor his maidservant, nor his ox, nor his ass, nor any thing that is thy neighbour's.

Just like every government entity on the entire planet, God also has laws.

In fact, his instructions are collectively known as "the law", and in 1 John 3:4 sin is defined as "the transgression of the law"...

4 Whosoever committeth sin transgresseth also the law: for sin is the transgression of the law.

Needless to say, all of us have broken God's law over and over and over again.

If you look back through your life, there are lots of things that you are deeply ashamed of doing. Some of them others may know about, and others you probably hope that nobody ever finds out about.

And just like in every other legal system, when God's law is broken there is a penalty to be paid.

173

If you went out today and murdered someone and the police caught you, would you expect to go free?

Of course not. Instead, you would probably be anticipating spending most of the rest of your life in some nightmarish prison somewhere.

Well, God is the perfect judge, and He knows every single one of the evil things that you have ever done.

Someday you will stand before Him, and none of your secrets will be hidden.

That thought should chill you to your core.

Are you ready to be held accountable for all of the wicked things that you have ever done?

The good news is that someone else has already paid the price for every sin that you have ever committed.

God loves you so much that He sent His only Son to die on the cross to pay the penalty for the sins of the entire world.

You are probably familiar with John 3:16...

16 For God so loved the world, that he gave his only begotten Son, that whosoever believeth in him should not perish, but have everlasting life.

The first time that Jesus came into this world, it was a rescue mission. He willingly allowed Himself to be nailed to a wooden cross to pay the penalty for all of our sins.

As it says in Romans 5:8, Jesus sacrificed Himself for us even though we did not deserve it...

8 But God commendeth his love toward us, in that, while we were yet sinners, Christ died for us.

We were stone cold guilty, but the Son of God died in our place.

Being fully man, Jesus could die for the sins of humanity.

Being fully God, Jesus could die for an infinite number of sins.

He was mocked, He was beaten, He was scourged ruthlessly and He was nailed to a wooden cross. He was totally innocent, but He was willing to suffer and die because He loved you that much.

Three days and three nights after He died, Jesus proved that He is the Son of God by rising from the dead.

In fact, Jesus specifically told His followers that this would happen well ahead of time. This is what Matthew 12:40 says in the Modern English Version...

40 For as Jonah was three days and three nights in the belly of the great fish, so will the Son of Man be three days and three nights in the heart of the earth.

If there was any other possible way for us to be reconciled to God, Jesus would not have had to die on the cross. He could have just told us to follow one of the other ways to get to heaven. But there was no other way. The death of Jesus on the cross is the only payment for our sins and He is the only way that we are going to have eternal life. In John 14:6, Jesus put it this way...

6 Jesus saith unto him, I am the way, the truth, and the life: no man cometh unto the Father, but by me.

But it is not enough just for you to intellectually understand that

Jesus is the Son of God and that He died on the cross for your sins.

The Scriptures tell us that we must individually commit our lives to Jesus Christ as Savior and Lord. When we give our lives to Jesus, He forgives our sins and He gives us eternal life...

"But as many as received him, to them gave he power to become the sons of God, even to them that believe on his name" (John 1:12).

"That if thou shalt confess with thy mouth the Lord Jesus, and shalt believe in thine heart that God hath raised him from the dead, thou shalt be saved." (Romans 10:9).

So precisely how does someone do this?

It is actually very, very simple.

The Scriptures tell us that it is through faith that we enter into a relationship with Jesus Christ. Ephesians 2:8-9 tells us the following...

8 For by grace are ye saved through faith; and that not of yourselves: it is the gift of God:

9 Not of works, lest any man should boast.

Entering into a relationship with Jesus is an act of faith. It means renouncing all of your sins and making Him your Savior and Lord. Just to know intellectually that Jesus died on the cross and that He rose from the dead is not enough to become a Christian. Having a wonderful emotional experience is not enough to become a Christian either.

You become a Christian by faith. It is an act of your will.

And if you want, you can do that right now.

Are you ready to make a commitment to Jesus Christ?

If you are ready to invite Jesus into your life, it is not a complicated process.

Just tell Him.

It doesn't matter if you say everything perfectly or not. What really matters is the attitude of your heart.

If you are ready to become a Christian right now, the following is a prayer that can help you express that desire to Him...

"Lord Jesus, I want to become a Christian. I know that I am a sinner, and I thank You for dying on the cross for my sins. I believe that you are the Son of God and that you rose from the dead. I repent of my sins and I open the door of my life and ask You to be my Savior and Lord. At this moment, I commit my life to You. Thank You for forgiving all of my sins and giving me eternal life. Take control of my life and make me the kind of person that You want me to be. From this point on, I will live my life for You. Amen."

If you are ready to enter into a personal relationship with Jesus Christ, then I invite you to pray this prayer right now. Jesus will come into your life, just as He has promised to do.

If you have invited Jesus to come into your life, you can know with 100 percent certainty that you have become a Christian and that you now have eternal life. In 1 John 5:11-13, the Scriptures tell us the following...

"And this is the record, that God hath given to us eternal life, and this life is in his Son. He that hath the Son hath life; and he that hath not *the Son of God hath not life. These things have I written unto you that believe on the name of the Son of God; that ye may know that ye have eternal life".*

Do you understand what those verses mean?

If you have invited Jesus Christ into your life, your sins are forgiven and you are now a member of the Kingdom of God.

In other words, you will live forever.

Our society has trained us not to think about what happens to us after we die, but the truth is that we are all going somewhere. In John 3:36, Jesus made this exceedingly clear...

"He that believeth on the Son hath everlasting life: and he that believeth not the Son shall not see life; but the wrath of God abideth on him."

Is there anything that you currently have that is so valuable that you wouldn't be willing to give it up for the opportunity to live forever?

I know that I have shared a lot of bad news in this book, but ultimately this book also contains the best news that you could ever possibly get, because I am sharing with you how you can have eternal life.

And no matter how bad things get in this life, if you know Jesus then you win in the end.

As Hal Lindsey once said, a new world is coming, and those of us that have been saved have a future that is brighter than we can possibly even imagine right now.

But as the rest of this book explains, we have got some very challenging years that we must endure first.

If you have decided to become a Christian, you are going to need some help in taking the very first steps in your new life. The following are four important keys that are critical to the spiritual growth of any Christian…

#1) The Bible – If you do not have a Bible you will need to get one and read it every day. It is God's instruction book for your life.

#2) Prayer – Prayer does not have to be complicated. Prayer is simply talking with God, and God wants to hear from you every day. As you grow, you will discover that prayer is an absolutely indispensable spiritual tool.

#3) Fellowship – The Scriptures very clearly tell us that we all need each other. Find a fellowship of local Christians that believe the Bible and that sincerely love one another. They will help you grow in your new faith.

#4) Witnessing – Tell others about the new life that you have found in Jesus Christ. Helping even one person find eternal life is of more value than anything else that you could ever accomplish in this world.

If you have made a decision to invite Jesus Christ to come into your life, I would love to hear from you. You can contact me at the following email address…

TheEconomicCollapseBlog @ Hotmail.com

If I could pick any time in human history to be alive, it would be right now. The years ahead will be a period of immense darkness, but they will also be an opportunity for us to do absolutely unprecedented things. There has never been a time like this before, and there will never be a time like it again. The entire history of humanity has been building up to this moment, and the greatest adventures of all time await those that are totally committed to our King.

All over the world, God is now raising up a Remnant that will keep His commandments, that will boldly proclaim the gospel to the whole world, and that will see that message supernaturally confirmed by the power of the Holy Spirit just like the very first believers in Jesus did. This is already happening all over the globe even though no organization is in charge of it. This Remnant is described in Revelation 12:17 and Revelation 14:12, and you can be a part of it.

This is the time of the final transition of the church. God is bringing things full circle, and that is going to change everything.

The Remnant of the last days is going to do things the way that Christians in the first century did things. Have you ever wondered why so many Christian churches today do not resemble what you see in the Bible? Well, the sad truth is that over the centuries churches got away from doing the things that the Scriptures tell us to do, but now God is restoring all things. Without God we can do nothing, but with God all things are possible.

Today, we have such an amazing opportunity. During the first century, there were only about 200 million people on the entire planet. Today, there are more than 7 billion. That means that the population of the world is about 35 times larger today than it was back then.

I believe that millions upon millions of souls will be brought into the Kingdom during the 7 year apocalypse, and I encourage you to be a part of what is happening.

As natural disasters, war, pandemics and economic troubles shake the globe, people are going to be looking for answers. Countless numbers of people will have their lives totally turned upside down and will be consumed with despair. Instead of giving in to fear like everyone else, it will be a great opportunity for the people of God to rise up and take the message of life to a lost and dying world.

Yes, believers will face tremendous persecution during the years that are in front of us. The world absolutely hates the gospel, and the Bible tells us that many Christians will be hunted down and killed for what they believe.

But those that have read the end of the book know that we win in the end. The Bible tells us that Jesus is coming back, and He will reign forever and ever.

In these last days, those that have a passion for God and a passion for reaching the lost are going to turn this world absolutely upside down for Jesus.

The Scriptures tell us that "there is joy in the presence of the angels of God over one sinner that repents." We are in a great battle for souls, and every victory is a major victory.

In fact, the Bible tells us that when even a single person makes a commitment to Jesus Christ, there is tremendous celebration in heaven.

As millions upon millions of precious souls are brought into the Kingdom in the years ahead, what do you think the atmosphere in heaven is going to look like?

Yes, darkness and evil will also prosper greatly in the days ahead. A one world government, a one world economy and a one world religion are coming. This one world system will utterly hate the

Remnant and those that support it will try to crush us with everything that they have got.

It is going to take great strength and great courage to stand against the one world system during the times that are approaching. You have the opportunity to be a part of a greater adventure than anything that Hollywood ever imagined, and in the end it may cost you your life.

But in Revelation chapter 2, Jesus promises us that if we are faithful unto death that He will give us a crown of life.

For those of us that have a relationship with Jesus, we know that we have the ultimate ending to our story. Jesus has forgiven our sins and has given us eternal life, and nobody can ever take that away from us.

Life is like a coin. You can spend it any way that you want, but you can only spend it once.

Spend your life on something that really matters.

If you enjoyed this book, I would encourage you to also follow my work online. I have written thousands of articles over the years, and you can find them on the following websites that I regularly update...

The Economic Collapse Blog: http://theeconomiccollapseblog.com/

End Of The American Dream: http://endoftheamericandream.com/

The Most Important News: http://themostimportantnews.com/

Thank you for taking the time to read this book all the way to the end. I would love to hear any feedback that you may have. Just like everyone else, I am always learning.

I will be praying for you and for all of those that read this book.

May the Lord bless you and keep you.

May the Lord make His face shine upon you and be gracious to you.

May the Lord lift up His countenance upon you and give you His peace.

Amen.

ABOUT THE AUTHOR

Michael Snyder

Michael Snyder is a graduate of the McIntire School of Commerce at the University of Virginia, and he has both a J.D. and an L.L.M. from the University of Florida Law School. He worked as an attorney in the heart of Washington D.C. for a number of years, but he left that career to prepare the way for the return of the Lord as a voice crying out in the wilderness.

From his home in the mountains, Michael's work touches millions of people all over the globe. His previous books include Lost Prophecies Of The Future Of America, The Beginning Of The End, Get Prepared Now, and Living A Life That Really Matters. By purchasing these books you help to support the work that he is doing. Michael is also known for the thousands of articles that he has published on The Economic Collapse Blog, End Of The American Dream and The Most Important News. Those websites have collectively been viewed more than 100 million times, and Michael's articles are also republished on dozens of other prominent websites all over the globe.

BOOKS BY THIS AUTHOR

Lost Prophecies Of The Future Of America

For decades, people all over the world have been having super-natural experiences in which God has shown them the future of America. These prophecies are incredibly detailed, they are remarkably consistent, and some of them have already started to come to pass. Unfortunately, most people have absolutely no idea that these prophecies actually exist. Most of them have been buried under the sands of time and have long been forgotten, but now the events that these prophecies foretold are starting to happen right in front of our eyes.

The Rapture Verdict

The worst times in all of human history are coming, and what Michael Snyder has uncovered is this book has dramatic implications for every man, woman and child on the entire planet. The Rapture Verdict is likely to become one of the most controversial Christian books in decades, and it addresses many of the hottest questions being debated today...

-Will Christians have to go through all of the chaos described in the book of Revelation?

-Is the judgment of God coming to America?

-Are we on the verge of entering the Great Tribulation?

-What is "the parousia", and how does that ancient Greek word completely shake up conventional theories about the rapture?

-Does the rapture come before, after or somewhere in the middle of the Tribulation?

-Why are millions of Christians in the western world going to become extremely angry with their pastors?

-Do the Biblical festivals provide us with a prophetic template for the events surrounding the second coming of Jesus Christ?

-Will this be the generation that witnesses the rise of the Antichrist and the Mark of the Beast?

-Is the organized church in danger of missing out on the greatest move of God the world has ever seen?

The Beginning Of The End

The Beginning of the End is the first novel by Michael T. Snyder, the publisher of The Economic Collapse Blog. If you want to know what things in America are going to look like in a few years, you need to read this book. The Beginning of the End is a mystery/thriller set in the United States in the near future. It is a time of unprecedented economic collapse, deep political corruption, accelerating social decay, out of control rioting in the cities and great natural disasters. In the midst of all of this chaos, a former CIA agent, a respected financial reporter and a blogger that takes his prepping to extremes all find themselves dropped into the middle of an ancient conflict between two shadowy international organizations. The three of them are absolutely horrified to discover that one of those shadowy international organizations is planning to hit New York City with the largest terror attack in U.S. history. The goal is to throw the entire country into chaos, but who will get the blame? A series of incredibly shocking twists and turns ultimately culminates in a wild cross country chase that leads up to a surprising ending that most readers will not see coming.

Living A Life That Really Matters

Deep inside all of us is a yearning to live a life that is filled with meaning and purpose. We all want to feel good about our lives, and we all want something to look forward to when we get out of bed in the morning. As little children we were filled with hopes and dreams for the future, but for so many of us those dreams have long since faded. Instead, many of us drag ourselves through life feeling down, depressed and defeated.

In this book Michael Snyder is going to share with you what he has learned about living an overflowing life. We were designed to love, to laugh, to discover, to create and to live lives that are filled with passion. Unfortunately, so many of us have bought into lies that have enabled the enemy to steal all of that from us. No matter how bad things may seem right now, God can take the broken pieces of your life and turn them into a beautiful thing. But you have got to be willing to break your old patterns and start doing things that will produce good fruit in your life. This book will help you to do that.

Made in the USA
Coppell, TX
08 August 2023

20118057R00107